Big Book of Trivia

997 Random Fun Facts, Trivia Questions, Sports Trivia, Pub Quiz Stuff, and Anecdotes to Amaze Your Family and Friends

Adicus Abbott

Copyright 2016 © Adicus Abbott

Published in the United States

ISBN-13: 978-1530706365

ISBN-10: 153070636X

Table of Contents

Dedication

Facts are rarely just facts.

In fact, the facts in this book reveal a lot about how we name things, how we confuse and jumble things, and what we think of each other.

With that in mind, I want to dedicate this book to all the trivia purists out there, the intrepid and hardcore pub quiz maestros in search of a slam dunk edge, and even the casual information junkies who simply want to dip into this book of random fun facts in search of a moment's diversion.

This book's for you!

Author's Note

Thank you for reading the *Big Book of Trivia*.

I first realized the joy of reading fact books when I discovered the *Guinness Book of World Records* somewhere around the 6th grade.

The major appeal of this book was the idea that you could flip the pages, and learn something at random…without having to start on the first page and read it sequentially like a traditional book.

But something was missing! What is missing from most fact based books is the story behind each fact.

When I set out to write this book, I wanted to focus on adding a brief story or anecdote to each fact. I didn't succeed in adding a story to each fact, but I hope you'll find enough stories in this book to make it a unique and interesting read.

Thanks again for reading my book.

Adicus Abbott

"To the trivia geek, facts others scorn, belittle, or otherwise ignore, are critical pieces to a huge puzzle—called life. Dispose of them at your own peril."

Adicus Abbott

997 Fun Facts and Anecdotes

In the world of playful plurals, the collective noun for a group of crows is a *murder*. Which may leave you wondering…what do scientists call a row of crows on a telephone line…*murderer's row*?

****

Early missionaries to South America discovered the joys of drinking hot chocolate, and in particular around the year 1550, one convent of nuns became so enraptured with the intoxicating drink, the church had to recall them to Europe. Shortly thereafter, the Catholic Church created rules and guidelines dictating the proper and improper use of chocolate.

To this day a popular cocktail featuring hazelnut and vanilla, used in the nun's chocolate drink, is called *The Hot Nun*.

****

Speaking of nuns, the famous lover Casanova was imprisoned after insulting the church by announcing the hottest women in Venice were all nuns. Casanova eventually escaped from prison, but was unable to return to his beloved city of Venice. He died in exile.

In 2005 Heath Ledger played a very convincing aficionado of love in the movie *Casanova*, directed by Lasse Hallstrom.

****

Bats are mammals and give birth to live babies. A bat delivers her baby on the fly and must swoop down and catch the newborn baby before it hits the ground.

****

Adult Americans watch over 33 hours of television per week, and while most of us have cable or satellite access to an average 189 channels, the vast majority of these channels are shopping networks, or stations that specialize in broadcasting reruns of *Gilligan's Island*.

****

A Dutchman named Cornelius Drebbel invented the first working submarine in 1620. Centuries later, Confederate forces built a submarine called the *H.L. Hunley* in 1863, and went on to lose 21 sailors attempting to use her in the American Civil War.

****

The entire city of Venice, Italy was built on a salt marsh that was originally used as a point of refuge from marauding warlords.

****

Michelangelo was highly criticized for giving the Sistine Chapel portrayal of Adam a navel. Technically speaking, God's creation of the first human would not have been born from a woman, and would not therefore, require an umbilical cord.

****

Out of money? Don't feel like you're alone. Many of us have "more month than money," but according to a Bankrate survey of 4,000 adults, two-thirds of us have less than $1,000 in savings, and one out of four of us don't even have a savings account.

Early on in my married life I was an airman in the U.S. Air Force. Pay grade wise, I was about one notch above a buck private. But thanks to my wife, I learned a few things about money and putting something away for a rainy day.

It started with a complaint from my wife, who claimed the lines and crowds at the commissary (on base grocery store) were unbearable on pay day. As it turns out, military guys are just like civilians…the further it is from pay day, the broker we all are. So naturally, by the time pay day came around, everybody on base was making a beeline for the commissary to restock the pantry and fridge.

My wife's cracking smart idea was to start saving a little bit of each paycheck until we had enough in savings to equal at least one pay check. When we had raised the funds, she was then able to start shopping days before pay day, when the commissary aisles were empty and the vast majority of the families on base were home eating the stuff nobody eats unless they're broke.

Eventually, the desire to avoid the pay day rush taught us the discipline to save…and everything was cozy and warm until the fall of 2008.

Think back to what was happening that fall. John McCain and Barack Obama were competing for George Bush's job, and the economy was teetering on the edge of collapse.

In the span of about three months, many Americans (including myself), lost over 40% of their nest eggs when the stock market went south, and to add insult to injury, the value of our home dropped by over 50% when one out of four houses in my neighborhood were lost due to foreclosure.

It helped to have money in a savings account, but for 62% of Americans, it was business as usual. You may find these government statistics, from agencies like the Census Bureau and the Bureau of Labor Statistics, interesting:

- The median household income in 2008 was $55,380. In 2015, the median income was $53,657.
- The labor participation rate fell to a record low of 62% in September, 2015. Meaning 38% of working age adults in America were unemployed.
- While 38% of the labor force is not at work, the published unemployment rate hovers around 5.2%. This number is much lower than the labor participation rate because it only reflects the percentage of adults who are currently asking for unemployment benefits.
- In 2008, over 70% of adult Americans owned their own home. In 2015, this number dropped to 63%.
- As of 2015, the federal minimum wage rate was $7.25, the same since 2009. With inflation kicked into the equation, the effective earnings of a minimum wage worker in America was the same as it was in 1969.
- Nationwide, Americans lost over $3 trillion in home value in 2008. For those of us silly enough to invest in the stock market at the time, nearly $7 trillion in value evaporated overnight.

****

Between the years 1793 to 1837, the American penny was made from pure copper. The first release of pennies into circulation consisted of 11,178 cents, or about $111. As of 2015, the U.S. Mint stamps about 13 billion pennies annually.

****

Austrians lead the world in alcohol consumption, with over 12 liters of alcohol consumed annually by persons over the age of 15. In comparison, Americans consume 8.6 liters annually. Interestingly, Austria is five times stricter with drunk driving rules for drivers with less than two years of driving experience. Apparently, experience makes a difference when it comes to driving under the influence.

****

The Amazon River is 150 miles wide where it dumps into the Atlantic Ocean.

****

Everybody loves a good kudo. After all, the pursuit of compliments is one of man's primary objectives in life. According to the lexicon of all things literary, the word *kudo* comes from an ancient Greek word of similar sound. But it was not until the 1920s that theater critics made the word popular when they used the word to praise a play or theatrical performance.

****

A South American snake known as the Eyelash Viper has scales over its eyes that resemble eyelashes. But don't be transfixed by its beautiful eyes, this snake is poisonous.

****

Civil War food contractors were notorious profiteers. At one point the addition of extra ingredients, such as sawdust and dirt, to ground coffee became so rampant, Abraham Lincoln ordered that all coffee be shipped to soldiers in the field in whole bean form. Early each morning the sound of thousands of musket butts being stomped into pots or onto tree stumps to crush the beans alerted the Confederate soldiers that the Union army was awake.

Over 600,000 Americans died during the Civil War, but ironically, around 400,000 of those deaths can be attributed to non-battle related illnesses and injuries. Here are some of the common causes of death among Civil War soldiers...

1. Poor nutrition
2. Exposure to weather
3. Lack of medical care
4. Lousy personal hygiene
5. No access to fresh water
6. Garbage piled in camp
7. Spoiled food
8. Bug infestations

A decent pair of boots, new socks, and a quilt from home dramatically improved a soldier's survival rate.

****

Operation Overlord was the codename assigned to the allied invasion of continental Europe on June 6, 1944.

****

Many totem poles carved by Native Americans in the Pacific Northwest feature creatures resembling Big Foot.

****

A prized treat for bears coming out of hibernation is skunk cabbage. This malodorous plant is famous for its fiber content and helps the bear clean out its digestive tract after being clogged for months.

****

During the Middle Ages people believed the earth was encased in a crystal sphere, like a dome. At the advent of the cannon, believers in the crystal dome idea feared an errant cannon ball could shatter the dome, destroying life on earth.

****

Christopher Columbus reportedly sighted three UFOs emerge from the ocean. According to his logbook, he witnessed three bright lights emerge from the dark waters and fly into the sky.

Skeptics attribute his sighting to St. Elmo's fire, which is technically an electrical charge, like lightning, that occasionally collects on the tall masts of ships at sea. St. Elmo is the patron saint of sailors, and any sighting of St. Elmo's fire was considered a blessing from the saint.

****

At one point, Roman soldiers were paid in salt, which was a valuable commodity they could use as barter. The word *salary* is derived from the word *salt*.

****

Americans eat over 50 billion hamburgers per year, which adds up to about 40% of all sandwiches eaten. In an affront to Germany during World War I, patriots were asked to call hamburgers *Liberty Sandwiches*.

****

Speaking of sandwiches, the concept of eating meat and veggies wedged between two slices of bread comes from John Montagu, the Earl of Sandwich in the 1700s. Apparently, Montagu loved to gamble and routinely asked for his dinner to be served between two slices of bread to facilitate eating and playing cards at the same time.

Now, thanks to the sandwich, we can gamble, drive, or watch football without having to scrounge around for a fork.

Bonus Fact: The Hawaiian Islands were originally named the Sandwich Islands by Captain James Cook in 1778.

****

With a name like the Lone Ranger, you would expect a person to spend his days alone, roaming the prairie on horseback, and wondering why the good folks back home never bothered to write. Instead, the Lone Ranger of western lore was constantly harassed by assorted cattle rustlers, villains, whining pioneers, and even a pesky sidekick named Tonto. Just how far into the sunset must a guy ride to get away from it all?

****

The comedy *Idiocracy* creates a dystopian future world by claiming the world's population became less intelligent over the generations, leading to a world of idiots, led by even bigger idiots. The basic premise of this movie suggested educated and successful people delayed having children, while the less educated and less successful elements of society reproduced with random and frequent abandon.

The truth is, the movie got it right. According to birth rate averages in America, nonprofessional women are five times more likely to have an unplanned pregnancy than professional women.

****

The Caspian Sea, located on the southern border of Russia, is the largest lake in the world. While the Caspian is saltwater, it still qualifies as a lake due to its "landlocked" status. The Caspian is 142,000 square miles in area. Compare this to Lake Superior, at 31,700 square miles.

If you encounter this fact in a pub quiz, be careful to note the distinction between freshwater and saltwater. A common quiz question asks: Name the largest freshwater lake in the world. In this case, the correct answer is Superior; however, if the question simply asks you to identify the largest lake, Caspian is the correct answer.

Subtle semantics of this nature are favorite ruses used in pub quizzes. Pay attention, and remember: Critical thinking and precision in language are your keys to success in pub quizzes.

****

Prior to dying at the age of 42, Jon Brower Minnoch was considered the largest human being on the planet. At his peak weight, he weighed 1,400 pounds. To Jon's credit, he also holds the record for weight loss and lost over 900 pounds...presumably through diet and exercise.

While an average 35% of adult Americans are considered overweight or obese as a result of poor diet and exercise regimens, a body weight like Jon's is often associated with an illness or genetic disorder.

In the airline industry, early standards for seating and passenger capacity were established using an average passenger weight of 170 pounds. Sadly, it is getting more and more difficult for most of us to fit in the narrow spaces airlines allot our above average backsides.

In a clever and politically correct sign of the times, I almost exceeded the allowable weight for a zip line ride. Prior to paying for a ride on the zip line, riders are required to weigh in. But the scale does not reveal a weight, and the zip line proprietor does not reveal the maximum allowable weight. They simply have a green and red zone painted on this huge grain scale. If the needle touches the red, you're quietly invited to take a hike, presumably to their conveniently located pub and sandwich shop next door. Using a handy magnifying glass, the zip line proprietor determined there was indeed a gap between the needle and the red zone when I weighed in.

****

Albert Einstein reportedly had an IQ of 160. Recently, a teenaged girl named Lydia Sebastian, scored 162 on an officially administered IQ test.

A person of average intelligence has an IQ of 100, with the degrees of intelligence moving towards genius increasing in 15 point increments (the standard deviation of IQ scores). Genius level intelligence is set at 140 and above…although a score in the 120-139 range is generally sufficient to figure out how to find and download incredible books like this one on Amazon Kindle…thus proving you are indeed genius material. Statistically, less than 1% of the population scores in the 140 or above range.

****

Human beings are amazingly arrogant. In the grand scheme of the entire universe, we are convinced that not only are we alone, but that our very own sun is the biggest ball of fire known to creation. Sadly, where size matters, our sun is a withered peanut compared to many stars in the universe, and one star in particular, VY Canis Majoris, is over one billion times the size of our sun. Now, that's a big ball of hot gas!

****

A skyscraper in Dubai known as the Burj Khalifa is the world's tallest manmade structure, at 2,722 feet. Using the standard of allowing 10 feet per story, this building could be 272 stories tall; however, once allowances are made for taller, atrium type floors, and antennae, this building has 163 accessible floors.

****

In the United States, the famous Observation Deck of the Empire State Building is on the 86th floor.

****

BASE jumping is a sport where people parachute off of things other than airplanes. The acronym BASE stands for: building, antenna, span, earth.

****

Saint Jude the Apostle is the patron saint for impossible, hopeless, and lost causes. Three other saints are recognized as benefactors to lost causes: Saint Rita, Saint Philomena, and Saint Gregory.

****

The most popular new baby name for girls born in 2015 was Charlotte. As for boys, the old Biblical name, Ezra, led the field.

****

The U.S. Secret Service is an Agency within the Treasury Department and is responsible for protecting the President of the United States. It was created on July 5, 1865, following the assassination of Abraham Lincoln. However, its original mandate was to investigate and stop counterfeiters. At the time, the federal government estimated up to one third of all currency in circulation was fake.

Following the assassination of President William McKinley in 1901, the Secret Service quietly assumed a more active role in protecting high ranking officials in the federal government.

In 2003, the Secret Service was moved out of the Department of Treasury, and made part of the newly formed Department of Homeland Security.

****

Up until the end of the Vietnam War, the U.S. Army routinely provided four cigarettes in each food ration pack.

****

During the Vietnam War, the number of U.S. soldiers on the ground peaked at around 550,000. Of those, less than 10% were assigned direct combat duties, with the bulk of soldiers performing support and maintenance roles.

Based on the nature of the Air Force's role in combat, less than 2% of the personnel on active duty in the Air Force perform a direct combat role.

****

At one time, Lucifer was considered God's right hand man. His name means "bringer of light." However, following his banishment from Heaven, Lucifer became known as Satan, the lord of darkness and evil.

During the Middle Ages, a musical chord called the Diminished Fifth, and also known as the Tritone or Devil's Chord, was banned by the Catholic Church in ecclesiastical music.

The beautiful song *Hallelujah* by Jeff Buckley includes the stanza, "They say there was a secret chord that David played and it pleased the Lord…It goes like this, the fourth, the fifth…" This is an apparent direct reference to the Devil's Chord.

The word hallelujah means "God be praised."

****

Hadrian's Wall was built by the Romans around 100 A.D. to separate the civilized Roman Briton area from the fierce "blue painted" Scottish warriors who lived north of the wall. The most common artifact found in the remains of the wall is discarded leather sandals from the Roman soldiers and their families.

A similar wall is portrayed in the television series, *Game of Thrones*, and not to be outdone by history or Hollywood, a controversial political initiative in America today involves building a wall to separate the Southwest border of America from Mexico.

****

Car alarms are not as new as you may think. The first car alarm was invented in 1913, and sounded an alarm if somebody tried to start the engine without first disarming the alarm.

Based on anecdotal evidence, the car alarm is useless, as less than 1% of alarm activations are the result of an actual crime. The general public has become aware of this as well, and generally ignore car alarms...or count it as just another source of noise in an urban environment.

****

Thinking of getting a pet parrot? Be careful, a Macaw Parrot may live over 100 years.

****

The Wells Fargo Bank got its start in the goldfields of California. In 1852 Henry Wells and William Fargo began offering secure transport of gold to banks in San Francisco, as well as banking services throughout Northern California and Sierra Nevada. Its six horse stagecoach became an instantly recognizable icon of the times.

****

In a sea trial voyage off the coast of Maine, the newest warship in the Navy, the Zumwalt, was called upon by the U.S. Coast Guard to assist in rescuing a fishing boat captain with a heart condition.

****

The United States purchased the territory known as Alaska from the Russians in 1867. The price: $7.2 million. William Seward was the Secretary of State at the time in charge of the negotiations. Seward came under harsh criticism for his attraction to Alaska, and opponents called the whole deal, *Seward's Ice Folly*.

****

Recycling plastic grocery bags is laudable, but researchers at Loma Linda University have found that up to 99% of used grocery bags contain bacteria, with some of them harboring e coli bacteria.

****

Your workplace is even worse than used grocery bags. Apparently, the average desktop has 400 times more bacteria than your toilet seat, and women's desks are typically dirtier than men's due to their more frequent handling of children and the use of make-up that transfers bacteria from the face to their hands.

The best way to protect yourself: Wash your hands more frequently.

****

The Greatest Show on Earth was a 1952 movie directed by the epic movie director Cecil B. DeMille. The movie depicts the inner workings of the Ringling Bros. and Barnum & Bailey Circus. The movie title comes from a marketing jingle created by the five original Ringling brothers who started the circus in 1884, and subsequently merged with Barnum & Bailey in 1919.

In 1957, Ringling Bros. and Barnum & Bailey Circus dropped the Big Top circus tent setup in favor of using existing venues, such as sports stadiums. Prior to this, their circus tents could hold up to 8,000 people...a fact that proved deadly on July 6, 1944.

On this date, the Ringling Bros. and Barnum & Bailey circus was performing in Hartford, Connecticut when its Big Top tent caught on fire. During the subsequent melee, 167 panicked guests died in the fire, and over 700 others were injured. At the time, circus tents were typically coated in paraffin wax to make them water proof. However, this practice also made their tents highly flammable.

Circus survivors were quick to note that in accordance with circus superstition, the cancellation of a July 5 performance due to bad weather, brought bad luck to the event. The exact cause of the fire was never confirmed; however a roustabout named Robert Segee confessed to starting the fire, but later recanted his confession. No charges were ever placed against Segee. Four circus organizers were charged and convicted for manslaughter, and were later pardoned. The circus paid out $5 million in damages to survivors.

This sad day in circus history is known as "The Day the Clowns Cried" in reference to a photograph of a popular clown holding a water bucket.

****

Big Ben is a four-faced clock located atop the Elizabeth Tower in London. It is the second largest four-faced clock in the world and was built in 1858.

The largest four-faced clock is located in Minneapolis, Minnesota.

****

In New York it is against the law to use an arm braced slingshot. The trademarked slingshot known as a Wrist Rocket is an example of an arm braced slingshot.

Shepherd slings, like the one used by David when he confronted Goliath, were legitimate military weapons in ancient battlefields. A skilled sling soldier could fire a projectile over 1,000 feet. Ballistics experts estimate David's projectile hit Goliath's head with a force comparable to a .45 caliber bullet.

****

8 of the top 10 tallest mountains in the world are in Nepal. The tallest, Mt. Everest, is 29,029 feet high. Sir Edmund Hillary is credited as the first man to reach the summit in 1953. Amazingly, his Sherpa guide, Tenzing Norgay, reportedly smiled and smoked a cigarette at the summit.

Next door, the widow maker K2 haunts the ambitions of many a mountaineer. At 28,251 feet, it is the second highest mountain in the world, but considered a more difficult and treacherous climb than Everest. To date, K2 has claimed over 80 lives and has never been summited in winter.

Many of the mountaineers who have died on K2 lie where they passed, and some of the frozen bodies remain as landmarks on the trail to the summit.

****

Philo Farnsworth first filed for a patent on his concept of projecting images in a cathode tube (television) in 1927. The predecessor to NBC broadcast the first live television show in 1928. Sadly, the Great Depression and World War II delayed widespread distribution of television sets, as well as the production of programming and building of broadcast stations, until the 1950s.

One of the first widely viewed and loved television programs was a morning news show. The *Today Show* has broadcast continually since 1952.

****

Turkeys are often mistaken as a gobble or a flock. But in fact, while domestic turkeys commonly found in grocery store freezers rarely fly due to their genetically designed and food induced weight, the correct playful plural for a group of turkeys is a *rafter*...which suggests turkeys in the wild prefer to lurk in high places...or at the very least beyond the reach of the farmer's wife.

Incidentally, while turkeys are commonly thought of as being stupid, they have a clever range of vocalizations, one of which can warn other turkeys of danger from a rattlesnake.

Here are some more collective nouns to amaze your zoologically minded sidekicks...

- A paddling of ducks.

- A gaggle of geese.
- A troop of apes.
- A peep of chickens.
- A brood of hens.
- A ballet of swans.
- And, a flamboyance of flamingoes.

****

Another highly appropriate collective noun is the word *mischief* for a group of rats. No surprise really, when you consider every rat you'll ever have the misfortune to meet is notoriously mischievous.

****

During the formative years of the United States, Benjamin Franklin argued in favor of selecting the wild turkey as our national emblem, as opposed to the Bald Eagle, which was seen as an eater of carrion and ranked among vultures for its character. Despite this distaste for eagles, the heraldic eagle has been recognized by many powerful empires throughout history…including Imperial Rome and Nazi Germany.

****

Cat gut strings for violins are made from sheep guts…not cats!

****

Currently, the following countries use an eagle on their flag or coat of arms: Albania, Armenia, Austria, Czech Republic, Ghana, Iraq, Mexico, Moldova, Montenegro, Nigeria, Palestine, Panama, Philippines, Poland, Romania, Russia, Serbia, Syria, United States, Yemen, and Zambia.

****

A zebra's stripes are like human fingerprints...no two are alike.

That said, I have no clue how a zebra family distinguishes themselves from other zebras in the herd.

****

On April 15, 1912, the unsinkable R.M.S. Titanic sank in the North Atlantic, taking 1,517 passengers and crewmembers to a watery death. R.M.S. stands for Royal Mail Ship. She was owned by the White Star Line. The ship was designed to carry 64 lifeboats, but on her fateful maiden voyage, only 20 lifeboats were onboard. R.M.S. Titanic was nicknamed, *The Ship of Dreams*.

****

During World War II, the *MV Wilhelm Gustloff* was torpedoed and sank in the Baltic Sea, claiming an estimated 9,400 lives. Most of the passengers were German evacuees from East Prussia.

In the Pacific, the *USS Indianapolis* was sank by Japanese forces on 30 July 1945 after delivering the first atomic bomb to the island Tinian. 879 U.S. servicemen died…many of them succumbing to shark attack in the days after the sinking. Due to its classified mission, U.S. Naval vessels in the area did not know of the crew's plight.

Captain Charles Butler McVay, commander of the USS Indianapolis, was court-martialed for a variety of trumped up charges that essentially accused him of negligence. Captain McVay was driven to a state of mental illness and eventually committed suicide in 1968.

****

Nostradamus saved thousands of lives by brewing a tea made from rose hips, which incidentally provided plague victims with much needed vitamin C. Ironically, when Nostradamus returned home from treating other villages hit by a 16th century plague, he found his own family had died of the same disease.

Interestingly, during the Middle Ages and Renaissance periods, villages often hired plague doctors to help treat and cure plague victims. Sadly, most plague doctors were in fact doctors who had been driven out of medical practice for lack of skill or knowledge. To their credit, plague doctors went into homes to treat victims, where others refused to venture.

During the Black Death plague in Europe between the years 1346 and 1353, an estimated 75-200 million people died, which represented roughly 60% of the population in Europe.

The popular children's playground song citing "ring around the rosy, pockets full of posies, ashes, ashes, we all fall down," is actually a derivation of a popular chant children recited during the Black Death plague, and directly referenced the fevered faces of victims, as well as the belief that posies in your pocket would ward off the deadly disease. As for the "ashes, ashes" part, the actual words were closer to achoo, achoo, suggesting the sound of a victim sneezing.

****

In 2010 a 60 mile traffic jam in Beijing, China, kept cars locked in place for up to one week…and in Tokyo, commuters have learned it is easier and faster just to walk or take a bicycle to and from work.

****

In Shanghai, china, a magnetic levitation bullet train travels at over 280 miles per hour.

****

The next time you play cards, take a close look at the Kings. Most standard card decks feature the *King of Hearts* without a moustache.

****

Ever been inside a casino and wondered what time it was? Most casinos go out of their way to hide clocks and create an atmosphere that helps you forget the passage of time…as you spend money.

****

Las Vegas is famous for its penny and nickel slot machines, which may lead you to wonder how casinos make money on penny bets. The truth is, a typical penny slot machine may offer up to 30 betting lines, with multiplying factors ranging from 1 to 10. Most slot players play all 30 lines with each bet, making the minimum bet 30 cents per spin. To win the jackpot almost always requires a $3.00 bet.

****

According to the FBI, the average bank robbery nets just under $5,000…and it's a federal offense. Despite the risks and low payout, 13 banks are robbed daily in the United States.

****

A 747 jetliner can carry 57,285 gallons of fuel. At just over 6 pounds per gallon, that equals over 360,000 pounds…and we haven't even added passengers and my daughter's luggage to the mix. To put it in perspective, just over one hundred years ago (1903), the Wright Flyer struggled to carry 140 pounds across a 120 foot stretch of windswept beach, near Kitty Hawk, North Carolina.

****

Americans receive over 4 million unsolicited telemarketing calls per day…most of which apparently target my area code!

****

Here's a challenge for you: Take any size sheet of paper and see how many times you can fold it in half. Reportedly, the maximum number of folds for any size sheet of paper is 7.

****

Americans drink over 44 gallons of soda per year. Since this is an average, chances are when non-soda drinkers are removed from the equation, the actual number would be much higher. This soda consumption contributes to our love of sugar. On average Americans consume over 120 pounds of refined sugar each year…compared to less than 4 pounds of sugar per year around 100 years ago.

****

James J. Braddock, also known as the *Cinderella Man,* won the World's Heavyweight Champion boxing title when he defeated Max Baer on June 13, 1935. However, the true champion of this story may be his mother…Braddock reportedly weighed over 17 pounds at birth.

****

In America, a family of four who earns less than $24,250 is considered poverty stricken. To put that in perspective, the median household income in America is $51,939. The statistical term *median* in this context means half the households in the U.S. earns more than $51,939 yearly, and half earn less.

****

In 1886 America's first serial killer, H.H. Holmes, purchased a drugstore in Chicago and converted it into a hotel to serve tourists visiting the 1893 World's Fair. The hotel was more like a house of horrors and locals refer to it as the *Murder Castle*, with booby traps and secret passageways designed to capture or kill its victims. Holmes confessed to killing 27 people, but police believe he may have killed over 200.

The original Holmes murder castle is now a bank. The basement area of the bank is used for storage and the bank's vault, and includes numerous walled off areas. Many bank employees given access to the area believe the basement is haunted.

Holmes' real name was Herman Webster Mudgett.

****

Tourists swimming in the waters around the Great Barrier Reef often experience mysterious symptoms similar to that of a jellyfish sting.

Experts believe the symptoms may be the result of exposure to box jellyfish spawn. The box jelly fish is considered one of the most toxic animals on earth, and merely brushing against one of the nine foot tentacles of a box jellyfish can be fatal.

****

The planet *Uranus* is not named after the god of urine or the god of bowel movements. In fact, the Greek god Uranus represented the sky. He is considered the king of the universe, and is the father of the Titans and the Cyclops.

So, how do you say the word *Uranus*?

Most of us try to pronounce it in a way that diminishes the anus connotation, choosing instead the pronunciation that suggests urine. Either way, the king of the universe got a bum rap on his name.

****

Based on extrapolations from the 2010 Census, the population of the United States in 2015 stood at 321 million. This number ranks the United States as the third most populous nation in the world, behind China and India.

****

In the book of Genesis, Esau sold his birthright to his twin brother Jacob for a bowl of lentil soup.

****

Ever heard the expression, "bird brain?" When it comes to ravens, you better think again. Ravens are considered the smartest birds, with an intelligence level equal to or greater than the domestic cat. In one case study, a college professor wore a scary mask while capturing a crow. Generations later, ravens on the campus still shouted warnings when participants in the study wore similar masks on campus.

While we're at it, if you're ever at the Los Angeles Zoo, be sure to catch the Bird Show, where you can watch ravens and crows snatch twenty dollar bills from the pockets of unsuspecting zoo visitors.

****

HTML stands for Hyper Text Markup Language, and is the common programming code used to create webpages.

****

The expression "your name is mud" was popularized when used to refer to the name of a doctor who treated John Wilkes Booth's leg injury following the assassination of Abraham Lincoln. However, it was first used in Britain decades earlier to imply a person was worthless. Like most myths and misconceptions, the myth is often more flamboyant or memorable than the truth. Doctor Samuel Mudd was subsequently imprisoned at Fort Jefferson, located in Key West, Florida. During an outbreak of yellow fever in 1867, Doctor Mudd was deemed a hero for saving hundreds of lives, and was later pardoned by President Andrew Johnson in 1869. Despite his heroics and apparent devotion to patient care, the words, "your name is mud" continue to carry an implied insult to its recipient.

****

The popular novel *Dances with Wolves* was written by a personal friend (Michael Blake) of Kevin Costner, who lived with the Costner family while he wrote it. The story originally featured the Cheyenne, but filming access to remote prairie land was only available with the Lakota Sioux.

****

In the book of Ezekiel, God calls Ezekiel a watchman for the house of Israel.

****

The Louvre Museum in Paris displays over 35,000 pieces of art, and receives over 9 million visitors per year.

However, don't bring your luggage to the museum. I can tell you from personal experience that the coat and baggage check window at the entrance of the museum will not accept packages or bags larger than a book bag…and for obvious security reasons the museum will not let you in with luggage in tow.

I can also advise you from personal experience that it is unwise to pay a helpful Parisian to *watch* your bags as you tour the museum.

****

High frequency trading, also known as HFT, on the New York Stock Exchange is known as a practice whereby traders move in and out of a trade within seconds. HFT accounts for up to 70% of the total share volume on the stock exchange, and while credited for making the market liquid, it also allows flash traders to move ahead of the market, putting normal, retail traders at a disadvantage.

The best known book on this subject is called, *Flashboys: A Wall street Revolt*, by Michael Lewis.

****

The National Rifle Association (NRA) is reticent to reveal its true membership levels, but anecdotal evidence suggests the total membership of the NRA ranges between 3.3 and 4.5 million.

Within the United States, the coveted 2nd Amendment protects the rights of citizens to own firearms. It is estimated by an international firm known as the Small Arms Survey, that there are over 270 million legally owned firearms in America. Cable News Network (CNN) estimates the number is closer to 310 million, and the FBI performs over 21 million firearm purchase background checks annually.

****

America is a nation of diverse peoples. According to the U.S. Census Bureau 77% of us arc White, 13% Black or African American, and 17% Hispanic or Latino. The numbers don't add up correctly due to some people self-identifying as "multi-race."

****

As of 2014, there were 20 million living veterans in America, making this a potent political group, capable of swaying elections towards politicians and issues relevant people with military backgrounds.

****

There are 110 million individual households in America, with an average of 2.6 people per household. Apparently, there are many households with legless or headless people running around.

****

In military parlance as recent as the Revolutionary War, a prostitute with venereal disease was referred to as a *Plague Ship* or a *Fire Ship* because she could potentially wipe out an entire Regiment. Somewhat pejoratively, a contagious woman was also known as, *Frenchified*. Of course, the man who gave her the disease, as well as the men who purchase her trade goods and subsequently spread the disease, are historically seen as victims.

****

Referring to a collection of birds as a flock is rarely an accurate use of the collective nouns for birds, unless used generically to describe a collection of birds of unknown name or type. In fact…

- Eagles come in convocations.
- Larks come in exultations.
- Peacocks come in ostentations.
- Parrots come in companies.
- Owls come in parliaments.
- Falcons come in casts.
- And nightingales come in watches.

But who dreams this stuff up? Scientists estimate there are over 8.74 million different species on Earth, with as much as 90 percent of the life forms on Earth uncatalogued. The cataloging of species in the animal kingdom is known as taxonomic classification.

Typical of science, the classification of species is an exact science...which makes sense, as any classification system that is not precise in its language is worthless. The classification process begins with a broad distinction between domains, and narrows to an exact classification within species. Here are the taxonomic classification steps in order:

- Domain
- Kingdom
- Phylum
- Subphylum
- Superclass
- Class
- Subclass
- Order
- Family
- Genus
- Species

Humans are notably part of the primate order, with homo and sapien referring to the genus and species, respectively.

****

The five kingdoms of Eukaryotes are: animals, plants, fungi, protozoa, and chromists. A Eukaryote is defined as a living organism with DNA, with the exception of some unlucky bacterium. And for the bonus round of any pub trivia contest, the definition of a chromist is not in this context a person who works with color; rather, a chromist is a living organism that possesses chlorophyll, including algae and water mold.

$$****$$

In music, especially opera, a vocalist's voice type is categorized by his or her predominant pitch. From highest to lowest there are 7 basic voice types: Soprano, Mezzo-Soprano, and Contralto for women; and, Countertenor, Tenor, Baritone, and Bass for men.

$$****$$

Cleopatra reportedly used a ruby as an IUD, and subsequently gave birth to five children. How she implanted and removed the ruby IUD is not known, but she sounds like an amazing woman. That said, perhaps rather than being remembered as the Queen of the Nile, Cleopatra's longstanding belief in the efficacy of her bejeweled contraceptive may qualify her as the *Queen of Denial.*

$$****$$

The world's population is 7.2 billion, with about 5 new babies entering the world every second. Among the nation's with the highest population, China leads the way with 1.3 billion people; India comes in a close second with 1.2 billion.

****

Black powder muskets used by pioneers and soldiers up to the Civil War typically shot a .50 caliber lead ball. The muzzle velocity for these guns was 1,200 feet per second. The modern rifle cartridge has a muzzle velocity of around 3,900 feet per second.

****

Muzzle velocity is the speed of the bullet the instant it leaves the barrel...typically measured in feet per second.

****

The first recorded pedestrian fatality happened in London, England in 1896. The victim apparently stepped off the curb into the path of a gas powered "horseless carriage." While the motor vehicle was only travelling at about walking speed, witnesses claim the pedestrian was so shocked to see the vehicle barreling down upon him, he "froze in place" and failed to move out of the way. During the autopsy, the coroner reportedly said, "I hope this is the last time this ever happens."

4,735 pedestrians died on American streets and roads in 2013. Despite the number of vehicle related traffic fatalities decreasing, the number of fatal pedestrian accidents continues to climb.

****

16% of all traffic related fatal accident victims in the United States are aged 65 and older. According to U.S. Census data, people over 65 make up 13% of the overall population, so this accident rate is somewhat proportional to their demographics, suggesting the urban myth that older drivers are more dangerous than younger drivers is just that...a myth.

****

Living *high on the hog*? This expression refers to the traditionally preferred parts of a hog being the shoulders. A similar expression, *upper crust*, has its origins in the tradition of social mores in Rome, and later in Europe, that required wealthy and aristocratic people to share their bread with people on the lower end of the socio-economic ladder. Loaves of bread were cut in half lengthwise, with the preferred upper portion going to the master, and the lower portion going to the servants and poor.

****

We all know the term *hooker* refers to a prostitute, but where did the word come from? During the Civil War, the Union General Joseph Hooker allowed "camp followers" that came to be known as *Hooker's Division.* Allowing young soldiers easy access to prostitutes did not sit well with the good folks back home, and political pressure eventually forced the Army to demote General Hooker.

****

Think your rent is too high? Nationwide, the U.S. Census Bureau claims the median rent is $920. That means half of us pay more than $920, and the other half pays less.

****

Somewhat related, during the Persian Gulf War a Marine unit stationed in Bahrain had the benefit of an enterprising female Marine who saw an opportunity to make some money while entertaining the troops. When she was eventually caught, she was immediately redeployed to the States, and her proceeds of over $12,000 donated to the unit's morale, welfare, and recreation fund.

****

Earthlings are proud of their moon, but the largest planet in the Solar System, Jupiter, is orbited by 63 known moons. The largest four of these moons are called: Io, Europa, Ganymede, and Callisto.

The popular candy bar, Snickers (a trademark name of Mars, Inc.), was named after the Mars' family horse.

And by the way, did you know all M&Ms (another Mars, Inc. trademark name) are born and raised in New Jersey? And as for the colors, nothing is left to chance. According to a *Modern Marvels* inside look at the world of chocolate, the color candied shells of M&Ms follow a formula:

24% Blue

20% Orange

16% Green

14% Yellow

13% Red

13% Brown

A popular urban myth once claimed the green dye used in green M&Ms was an aphrodisiac. There is no proof that this is true, but it does make the eating of M&Ms more enjoyable and enticing. Chances are, the truth of this urban myth is more likely related to the chocolate in an M&M, and not the food coloring.

****

Termites sleep during the day and work at night…which I suppose makes them graveyard shift workers.

****

Technically, bananas are herbs, not fruits. And contrary to popular belief, bananas do not come in *bunches*, they come in *hands*.

****

Chocolate was once consumed as a beverage, brewed with hot peppers and spices. The word *chocolate* comes from the Aztecs, who combined two of their native words (xococ and atl), meaning bitter water.

****

Don't have a tablespoon handy? Use a teaspoon. One tablespoon is equal to 3 teaspoons.

****

64% of American household are owner occupied. This means most of us live in the house we own. Of those homes, the median value is $175,700.

****

The first marathon was run by just one athlete. In 490 B.C., a Greek soldier named Pheidippides was called upon to deliver a message from Athens to Sparta in the Battle of Marathon. The distance travelled was 26.2 miles. According to eyewitnesses, the race organizers did not provide any feeding or first aid stations, and added insult to injury by not delivering on the promised commemorative t-shirt and participation medal.

****

Roughly 25% of all department store product returns and requests for refunds occur during the holiday shopping season, and among those returns, retailing experts estimate nearly $4 billion annually are fraudulent. So, the next time you get an ugly sweater or a housecoat that makes you look and feel like Grandma Moses, make your return within 30 days if possible, and don't be surprised if you're offered a cash value coupon instead of money.

A popular West Coast department store offers a no questions asked return policy, and while costly, routinely accepts returns for products they do not even sell in the interest of offering outstanding customer service.

****

On the dark side of retail operations, the *Annual Retail Theft Survey* claims 1 out of every 38 retail employees are charged with shoplifting from their employer.

＊＊＊＊

At any one time in America over 2.2 million people are incarcerated in federal, state, and local prisons...giving America the highest incarceration rate among developed nations, in the world. Ironically, Afghanistan has the lowest incarceration rate, despite the prevalence of terrorism and the heroin industry.

＊＊＊＊

James Watt is credited with inventing the first steam engine in 1763. However, Thomas Newcomen developed a working pressurized and piston driven steam engine in 1712; and in 100 A.D., the concept of using steam to propel a vehicle or turn a millstone was common knowledge.

＊＊＊＊

86% of Americans over the age of 25 have a high school diploma, and 29% of us have a college degree.

＊＊＊＊

Olive oil is traditionally graded according to its position in the sequence of pressings. To collect oil from olives, olives are harvested and placed in a pressing device. Each subsequent pressing of the olives produces a slightly different quality of oil. Extra virgin was the name given to the first cold pressing of the olives, and continues to be recognized as the highest quality olive oil. However, in today's methodologies, olives are ground to a paste, heated to 80 degrees Fahrenheit, and run through a centrifuge, and not pressed.

****

Soil taste is a term used by olive oil producers to describe the impact of soil and other contaminants on olives during processing. Obviously, the cleaner the olives prior to oil extraction, the lower the undesirable soil taste. Personally, I like my olive oil *sans* soil.

****

The fictional detective Sherlock Holmes, created by Sir Arthur Conan Doyle, lived at 221B Baker St. To this day, the Royal Mail continues to receive letters addressed to Sherlock Holmes.

****

Entomophobia is the fear of caterpillars. But don't laugh, quite a few of those cute critters crawling around your garden are toxic. Caterpillars have hollow bristles known as urticating hairs, and when touched, these bristles can exude poison. Most stinging caterpillars can cause localized pain when touched, but the giant silkworm moth caterpillar can kill you. In North America, the puss caterpillar is highly toxic and looks like a very cute ball of tan colored fur. Its sting feels like a bee sting, and can cause a host of horrible symptoms, including nausea, dizziness, difficulty breathing, and in some cases, death.

****

Despite the Affordable Care Act, also known as Obamacare, 12% of Americans have no health insurance.

****

The most venomous snake in the world is a sea snake with enough venom to kill 1,000 people. It's called the Belcher Sea Snake, and is located in the oceans around Southeast Asia and Northern Australia. The snakes are very docile and reported bites occur mainly among fishermen who catch the snake in their fishnets.

****

Former British Prime Minister Winston Churchill was famous for his wit and his drinking. But one of his more notorious charms was his skill in the art of the snappy comeback. That is, if you tried to insult Winston, chances were high the insult would come back at you in spades.

In one case, a political rival known as Lady Nancy Astor announced that if Winston were her husband she would put poison in his tea. Unperturbed, Churchill responded, "If I were your husband, I'd drink it."

In another verbal duel, Lady Astor noticed Churchill was intoxicated at a party. Reportedly, Lady Astor spouted, "Winston, you're drunk." To which Churchill responded, "Yes, I'm drunk. But you're ugly, and tomorrow I shall be sober."

Like I said, if you want to verbally assault somebody, make sure you don't get caught in your own bear trap.

****

On average, Earth is 93 million miles away from the Sun. It takes around 8 minutes for light from the Sun to reach Earth.

****

A light year is the distance light travels in one year. At a speed of 186,000 miles per second, light will travel over 5.8 trillion miles in one year.

****

The closest star to Earth (other than our Sun) is a 3 star system commonly known as Alpha Centauri, at a distance of 4.2 light years, or about 24 trillion miles.

If you ever find yourself answering this question in a pub quiz, be careful to note the distinction, "other than our Sun." Lacking that clarification, it is a trick question which trips quiz takers who forget that the Sun is a star.

****

Americans spend $1.6 trillion annually on healthcare services.

****

The average credit card debt in America is $5,047 per credit card user. Perhaps some of that debt has been accumulated by struggling fathers financing weddings. In America, the average wedding costs $26,444.

In a related statistic, one in five Americans claims they will go to their deathbeds in debt.

****

The Rubik's Cube was invented by Erno Rubik, a Hungarian sculptor and architect, in 1974. A kid named Collin Burns can solve the Rubik's Cube in less than 6 seconds.

****

The hull of the Mayflower ship that once transported pilgrims to Plymouth Rock is now a barn in Buckinghamshire, England. According to mariners, historians, and local farmers, she is a much better barn than she ever was a ship.

****

Been to the mall lately? Americans spend over $4 trillion annually in retail stores across the country.

****

Stephen King's first paying novel was *Carrie*, published by Doubleday in 1974. That same year, the Soviet Union drew up a battle plan to attack Manchester. Apparently, members of the KGB were Liverpool fans.

****

The most popular firearm among U.S. police officers is the Glock 22, .40 caliber semi-automatic pistol. Among homeowners, the most popular home defense weapon is a shotgun.

****

And speaking of weapons, your definition of a weapon may differ from that of the Transportation Security Administration (TSA). The TSA is responsible for airport and airline security. These are the people who ask us to empty our pockets and make us walk through metal detectors...and sometimes body scanners. It's a distasteful process for everyone involved.

According to TSA officials, in one East Coast airport alone, over 4 tons of prohibited items are confiscated from passengers per year. Items removed from carry-on bags include knives, corkscrews, and even the mixing blades from blenders.

Why anybody would need to bring a blender on an airplane is a mystery. Were they planning on making margaritas for all the other passengers?

****

Technically, a tomato is a *fruit*, and not a *vegetable*. It is a "New World" food, meaning it is native to the Western Hemisphere. It was first brought to Europe in the 16th century as a botanical curiosity—something to look at, but not eat.

Initially, Europeans referred to the tomato as the "poison apple," because people who ate the tomato died. The acidity in tomatoes may be toxic to some people with food allergies, but for the most part, tomatoes are not poisonous. However, it took nearly two centuries to convince Europeans to eat the fruit.

As it turns out, the villain in this story is not the tomato, but the dishes the tomatoes were served on. At the time tomatoes were first imported to Europe, the only people wealthy enough to eat this exotic fruit had a tendency to eat on pewter plates. Pewter plates were high in lead content, and the acid in tomatoes had an uncanny ability to leach the lead out of the plates and into the food. As a result, people who ate tomatoes off pewter plates were dying of lead poisoning.

****

Are elephants afraid of mice? Not really. As it turns out, ants are the true nemesis to elephants, as ants burrow in trees and when the elephants try to eat the leaves and branches of trees, the ants irritate the elephant's sensitive trunks.

Nature capitalizes on this innate fear for ants by deploying ants as tree bodyguards.

****

The first people to have indoor flushing toilets were the Cretans, who came up with the idea about 1,800 years before Christ. Interestingly, Queen Victoria is considered the first person in England to have indoor plumbing (other than perhaps the developer of the modern toilet, Thomas Crapper), and it was not until the creation of the Crystal Palace in London in 1851 that the general public had access to toilet facilities outside his or her own home…which begs the question: How did people survive going out to dinner and attending the theater without access to a toilet?

****

The American entrepreneur Harry Gordon Selfridge built the largest department store in London in 1909 and turned toileting into a marketing ploy by offering lady shoppers access to public toilet facilities. This innovation was unheard of at the time, and quickly gained in popularity as common sense prevailed over ancient tradition.

****

The average commute to work in America is 25 minutes.

****

The Palace of Versailles in France has over 700 rooms, and can entertain as many as 20,000 people at one time. However, when it was built, the palace did not have a single restroom. Instead of offering water closets to its guests, servants walked around the palace with chamber pots. Where and how the palace guests found the privacy to do their business is beyond the realm of my knowledge.

****

Flotsam and jetsam are not the same thing. Jetsam refers to stuff that has been intentionally thrown overboard or out of an aircraft to lighten the load, or somehow help a stricken ship from sinking. Flotsam, on the other hand, may be the same stuff as you would find in a collection of jetsam; however, flotsam has not been intentionally thrown overboard, and is the material left over from a ship or aircraft breaking apart or sinking at sea.

****

Most of us have no problem overloading our bodies with sodium, but when it comes to potassium, our bodies go begging. Supplements are rarely a good choice, as it is easy to supplement your way into excess with potassium. The best way to get potassium is by adding potassium rich foods to your regular diet. Of course, we could eat more bananas…but surprisingly, this famous potassium source is not necessarily our best choice, especially if you hate bananas or can't stand the wallop of fructose from a tropical fruit.

Here are some other great sources of potassium:

1. Sweet Potatoes
2. Tomatoes
3. Beet Greens
4. Yogurt
5. Carrot Juice
6. Fish
7. Orange Juice

****

A collection of space dust and rocks cannot become a round-shaped moon or planet until the gravitational pull of its own mass is sufficient to congeal the pieces into one mass. On average, a collection of dust and other particles must be at least 500 miles across for this gravitational magic to occur.

****

Rivers of floating trash move on oceanic conveyor belts across the planet's great oceans, comprised of anything manmade that can float, such as plastic bottles, cigarette butts, trash bags, and even pieces of furniture. In some cases, these floating islands of human waste can be miles across.

****

The consumption of opium was once known as *Riding the Dragon*—a veiled reference to the origin of the powerful drug.

While the illegal and uncontrolled use of opium is almost universally debilitating and harmful, it is the basis to a large variety of medicines, known as *opiates*, used in health care to this day.

****

In 1962, West Point Military Academy named a new barracks building after the Confederate Civil War General, Robert E. Lee. Lee graduated at the top of his West Point class in 1829, and served in the U.S. Army for 32 years. He was also the Superintendent of West Point from 1852 to 1855.

As a student at West Point, Lee was known as the *Marble Model*.

Leading up to the Civil War, Lee's home for 30 years was just across the Potomac River from Washington, D.C. By the end of the war, the home and the land around it had become what is now Arlington Cemetery.

****

Cotton mummy wraps were removed from Egypt by the boatload and used as rag material in the manufacture of butcher paper. The discolored linens are reputed to have led to the traditional brown color of paper bags used in grocery stores…although this may simply be the result of not bleaching the paper used for these bags.

Either way, there is evidence that a 19th century American explorer named Isaiah Deck travelled to Egypt around 1847 and was amazed by the vast quantity of mummy linen available in Egypt at the time. Deck observed this abundance of linen material (up to 30 pounds worth of finely woven linen per mummy) may be productively used in the manufacture of paper in the United States.

Sadly, the abundance of mummies in Egypt also prompted Egyptians to use dried mummies as firewood, and aristocrats in Europe routinely hosted "unwrapping" parties where they would entertain guests by unwrapping mummies. What happened to the desecrated bodies after the celebrations remains a mystery—which at the very least makes the "mummy hauntings" of many a child's sleepless nights, justifiable.

****

118 million Americans have jobs, and earn a cumulative $5.6 billion in wages.

****

The U-shaped and looped wire paper clip commonly used in offices around the world today was invented by Johan Vaaler, a Norwegian, in 1901.

Years later, the Post-it Note, a trademarked product of the American company 3M, was the accidental creation of a 3M employee named Art Fry, who first used the company's "low tack" adhesive in 1974 to attach small pieces of paper to a church hymnbook to mark specified pages without damaging or defacing the book.

****

The platypus is a rare mammal that lays eggs. It is indigenous to Australia and the male platypus has a unique spur on its back legs. But don't try to pick this rascal up! Its spurs are toxic and can cause serious illness and possibly death for people with weak immune systems.

Like most things in Australia, the platypus comes with a sting.

****

Of the 27 million business firms in America, women own 7.7 million of them, and 5.7 million firms are owned by minorities.

****

Thanks to Sam Heughan, the star of the *Outlander* television series, redheads are the rage. But this is nothing new, as research suggests Neanderthals carried the genetic marker for red hair.

It may have been the ice age, but there must have been some hot nights with all those red heads running around.

****

Another word for a penis is a *pizzle*.

****

A vehicle travelling at 60 miles per hour covers 88 feet per second.

****

For a long time people believed owls did not have an anus because of the way they typically regurgitate what is called an owl pellet. In fact, the owl pellet is a way for the owl to get rid of bones and skin it does not wish to digest. The owl digests its food and gets rid of the waste like any other bird.

****

In Native American mythology, the call of an owl at night presages death.

****

In a final nod to the power of owls, owls are considered among the oldest of all birds, and fossil remains suggest owls were calling dinosaur's names over 60 million years ago.

****

In the United States, the population per square mile is 87.4. In India, the population per square mile is 953.

****

The word *lunatic* is derived from the word *luna*, meaning moon. A common belief among humans to this day is that the gravitational forces of the moon, which impact tides and weather on earth, also impact the inner workings of the human mind—driving some people to lunacy.

An obvious symptom of rampant lunacy is howling at the moon. However, a more insidious and potentially entrapping act of moon madness, often mistaken for romance or love, is to stare at the moon while in the company of another.

****

One of the first inventors of the bicycle crashed on his creation and broke his collarbone.

****

The narwhal horn may be the source of the original myth regarding unicorns. Tricky sea merchants sold narwhal horns to wealthy landlubbers who displayed the horns as exotic artifacts.

****

The lowest point in North America is Badwater, in Death Valley, California. The elevation at this spot is 279 feet below sea level. Ironically, from this point, thirsty pioneers crossing the barren desert could look west to see the snow-capped mountains of the Sierras, as well as the highest point in the contiguous United States, Mt. Whitney, at 14,505 feet above sea level.

An annual ultra-marathon race challenges athletes to run from Badwater to a point known as the Whitney Portals, at a distance of 135 miles. The distance is not the major opponent in this race, as most runners drop out early due to July temperatures in Death Valley of approximately 120 degrees Fahrenheit, and blistering road surface temperatures in excess of 140 degrees.

****

The top 10 highest peaks in the United States are located in Alaska, with Denali, formerly known as Mt. McKinley, at 20,310 feet.

****

The deadliest job in the world is commercial fishing, with up to 200 deaths for every 100,000 fishermen and women.

One of the top 10 deadliest jobs you can have is to be a truck driver. So, the next time you see a trucker, give him or her a wide berth, wave, and be thankful there are men and women who drive trucks and deliver the food and fuel we need to survive.

****

The land area of United States is 3.5 million square miles. In terms of acreage, this equates to 2.2 billion acres, where 640 acres equals 1 square mile.

Much of the land west of the Mississippi River is divided into Sections. A Section is 640 acres. The original Homestead Act divided each Section in quarters, granting homesteaders one corner of a Section, or 160 acres.

Surveyors in the West use a process of describing property in terms of their Township, Section, and Quarters in a *rectangular* process. In the East, surveyors used an older English system known as *metes and bounds*. A property description in the East typically describes a property by defining the natural boundaries of a property, such as 300 feet along the northern bank of the Ohio River, 220 feet north to the large rock outcropping, and 422 feet east to the stake.

****

Do crocodiles cry? I've never gotten close enough to personally verify this, but according to intrepid crocodile lovers, croc's eyes weep while they eat. Apparently, this is not a result of remorse for killing its dinner; rather, it is a natural excretion through its tear ducts resulting from the vibration in its body as it enjoys its meal.

****

The word werewolf comes from the Old English word *were*, which means man.

Somewhat related, the scientific word for the transformative process of becoming a werewolf is lycanthropy.

****

A sphygmomanometer, technically a pulse meter, is a medical device used to measure a patient's blood pressure. The sphygmomanometer was invented by Samuel Siegfried Karl Ritter von Basch in 1881.

Fortunately, measuring your blood pressure using a sphygmomanometer is significantly less painful than pronouncing the name of its inventor.

****

The 728 foot iron ore freighter Edmund Fitzgerald went down in a Lake Superior storm on November 10, 1975. Her crew of 29 sailors went down with the ship. Prior to the sinking, the ship was known as the *Titanic of the Great Lakes* due to her size.

In his last known radio message seconds before the ship disappeared from radar, Captain Ernest McSorley stated, "We're holding our own." Gordon Lightfoot immortalized the disaster in his song title *The Wreck of the Edmund Fitzgerald* in 1976.

The Great Lakes are no strangers to maritime disaster. In another famous disaster known as the Christmas Tree Ship, the 123 foot schooner *Rouse Simmons* sank in Lake Michigan on November 23, 1912, loaded with Christmas trees headed for Chicago markets. 17 sailors died in the sinking, and divers visiting the crash site can still see the remains of Christmas trees neatly stack in her cargo hold.

Like the *Edmund Fitzgerald*, the *Rouse Simmons* went down in a November storm…a month that is known to locals going back for centuries, as dangerous in the Great Lakes region.

****

The expression "An Octopus's Garden" comes from the curtain of eggs surrounding a female octopus tending her eggs.

****

There are 157,724 miles of U.S. Numbered Highways in America. This does not include the countless state and local highways and backroads. Motoring across these highways are over 256 million registered vehicles…most of which are currently waiting in line at one of the 857 million stop signs currently erected across the nation.

****

Chinese dragons symbolize luck and good fortune; however, in the west a dragon symbolizes destruction, greed, and hording.

Mankind has three instinctive fears: snakes, big cats, and raptors. The dragon is a mythical creature that combines all three of these primal fears.

****

Thomas Edison is credited with the invention of the lightbulb in 1878. However, 23 different versions of the lightbulb had been invented as early as 1802 by other inventors. That said, Edison's use of a metallic coil (called a harp) placed in a glass vacuum created the first commercially viable lightbulb.

The first awe inspiring display of the lightbulb occurred during the World's Fair of 1893 in Chicago, where 100,000 incandescent lamps illuminated the night in a way never seen in the history of humankind.

****

Riparian water rights is a legal term for a landowner's rights to the use of water that prevents trapping and storing water that deprives other landowners of access to that water. For example, a landowner cannot trap or otherwise divert a river to prevent the water from following its natural course to the landowners downstream.

Riparian water rights were crucial in the west where scarce water resources must be allocated for multiple uses and multiple property owners.

****

Wolfgang Amadeus Mozart composed four pieces of music for the keyboard shortly after his fifth birthday. He went on to become the most accomplished composer of his time and is recognized to this day as one of the greatest music composers ever. Mozart was born in 1756 and died in 1791. Little is known of the exact cause of his death, but some believe he died of food poisoning. Mozart died in poverty and was buried in an obscure grave.

Don't know any Mozart? If you can hum the tune to *Twinkle Twinkle Little Star*, you are reciting one of his earlier works.

****

Of all the musical instruments used in an orchestra, the oboe is best noted for its stable pitch and clear sound. Because of this, most orchestra musicians tune their instrument to the oboe before the start of a concert.

****

In golf, a *birdie* is scored when the golfer scores one stroke less than the par for a specific hole. An *eagle* refers to two strokes under for the hole's par, and a *bogey* refers to hitting one stroke over the hole's par. In my case, a more familiar term is the *double bogey*, which means two strokes over par.

****

When ordering food, asking for something *a la carte* means to order an item separate from anything else. For example, if you asked for a grilled chicken dinner, a la carte, you would get the chicken, but not the potatoes and vegetables that may usually come with it.

****

The *In-N-Out* hamburger restaurant chain on the West Coast is popular among hamburger aficionados. But In-N-Out purists are also aware of a secret menu, where you can order things like *Animal Fries*, that come buried in the restaurant's secret sauce, cheese, and grilled onions.

Here's a recipe for a condiment similar to that used by In-N-Out:

½ cup Mayonnaise

2 tbsp Ketchup

2 tbsp Pickle Relish

2 tbsp White Wine Vinegar

1 tsp Lemon Juice

Salt to taste

Combine all the ingredients and refrigerate in a sealed container for use as needed. You may also want to lightly butter and grill your buns as well as your onions.

****

Food allergies are common, and in one form or another, most of us are probably allergic to one food type or another. Personally, I'm allergic to anything in the cabbage family. It tears me up, in a lactose intolerant way, making me poor company following even the smallest serving of corned beef and cabbage.

On a more serious note, peanut allergies top the list of children's food allergies, with the number of reported allergies tripling in the last 10 years. Sadly, this explosive trend has impacted the sale and consumption of nuts, but just because the word *peanut* ends with *nut*, peanuts are *legumes*…which means they are a bean, and not a nut.

****

There is a scene in the movie *Good Will Hunting* where Robin Williams criticizes Matt Damon's life experiences, claiming everything the Damon character knows comes from books, and not real life. To paraphrase Williams, "You can probably tell me that Michelangelo painted the ceiling of the Sistine Chapel, but you can't begin to tell me what the room smells like, or what it feels like to crane your neck back and stare at that beautiful ceiling."

I can tell you, the Sistine Chapel smells like you would expect a 600 year old plaster and brick building to smell. To me it smelled like wet cement and a touch of mildew. Added to that is the smell of hundreds of people from every corner of the world crowded together, sweaty from a long walk and hours spent standing in line, waiting for a chance to see one of the greatest art displays on the planet.

So, what does the Sistine Chapel smell like: cement, mildew, sweat.

But honestly, I had to think about it, because when I was there, I didn't notice. I was too busy staring up at the ceiling and wondering how a mortal man (Michelangelo) could possibly create what he created. Here are a few more facts you should know about the Sistine chapel:

1. The Sistine Chapel was built in 1477.
2. Michelangelo painted the ceiling between 1508 and 1512.
3. Approximately 5 million people visit the Sistine Chapel annually.
4. Michelangelo thought of himself as a sculptor, not a painter.
5. In the 1560s, Pope Pius IV commissioned the painting of fig leaves and loincloths to cover the nudes painted by Michelangelo. In the 1980s, some of these were removed during a restoration project.
6. Papal Conclaves assemble in the Sistine Chapel to elect new popes.

****

The most expensive coffee in the world is harvested from elephant dung. Apparently, the coffee growers feed the coffee beans to elephants, and then collect the castings after having been "processed" by the elephant's digestive tract.

Available in fine stores, everywhere!

****

According to the American Kennel Club, the Labrador Retriever is the most popular dog in America…as it has been for 21 straight years. But topping the list in popularity is not enough for this dog, as he has three times the number of registrations than the Golden Retriever, who comes in a distance second in popularity.

And this just in…the Labrador Retriever is the most popular dog in the UK as well.

So, why do people love the Lab, over all the other dog breeds available at your local pet shop or shelter?

Labs are sporty, energetic, loyal, and family friendly. Plus, they come in chocolate, black, and yellow.

But what I like best is their wash and wear fur. My Lab can spend half the day lounging neck deep in water in the bar ditch in front of my house, jump out, give it a good shake, and bolt for her reserved seat on the family couch…without stopping for a hair-do or towel.

You can't help but love a low maintenance dog who spends her day walking around with this look on her face that shouts, "Where can I find a face to lick?"

****

A baker's dozen is not 12, but 13. Throughout history many societies have imposed strict rules on commerce, and in the interest of protecting consumers from fraud, violation of these laws of commerce have led to draconian punishments. In the case of bakers selling loaves of bread, bagels, pretzels, and donuts, bakers traditionally added an extra loaf to ensure they counted correctly.

****

Speaking of the number 13, have you ever wondered why we consider 13, especially Friday the 13th as an unlucky number?

Friday the 13th is also known as Black Friday, and has been related to the crucifixion of Christ, as well as the arrest and subsequent execution of members of the Knights Templar by Phillip IV of France in 1307.

****

The superstitious fear of the number 13 is called *triskaidekaphobia*.

****

In China, the number 4 is considered unlucky because the sound of the word resembles the sound of the word for death.

$$****$$

Other than Black Friday referring to an unlucky date on the calendar, every year shoppers and business owners look forward to Black Friday, the traditional launch date for Christmas shopping in America.

In the context of business and accounting, the word "black" refers to the color of ink used in traditional bookkeeping. Red ink was used to denote losses; whereas, black ink was used to denote profits. Black Friday is the day when merchants can count on holiday shopping to lift them out of the red, and into the black.

$$****$$

Want the love of your life to say, "yes" to your marriage proposal? According to statistics from jewelry stores, the best day to propose is Christmas Eve. The winter holiday season is the best time to propose because the holiday season (at least for people in love) is a happy time, and couples are usually spending time with each other's family during this time. Also, by asking in December, it gives the bride enough time to plan a spring or early summer wedding. You should also know, the average diamond engagement ring will run you just under $6,000.

****

Pulmonary refers to lung function in the body, and cardiopulmonary refers to both the heart and lung. The first aid procedure abbreviated CPR stands for cardiopulmonary resuscitation.

****

The book of Genesis in the Holy Bible depicts God's creation of the universe and man. You may remember, God created the heavens and earth in six days, and chose to rest on the seventh. Here is what He created, by day:

Day 1: Created light and separated light from darkness.

Day 2: Created the heavens above and the water below.

Day 3: Created the oceans, land, and plants.

Day 4: Created the sun, moon, and stars.

Day 5: Created fish to fill the sea and birds to fill the sky.

Day 6: Created animals large and small, as well as humans.

****

The King James Holy Bible consists of 66 books. Compiling and translating the various historical documents used in the creation of the King James version of the Holy Bible was commissioned by King James of England in 1604. The 47 religious scholars assigned to the project completed their translation in 1611.

****

Zoologists and paleontologists now believe the bird is a descendant of the dinosaur. Theorists believe there was a mass extinction event, perhaps tied to the massive meteorite that hit the Yucatan Peninsula, 64 million years ago; however, this new belief suggests that while a mass die-off of dinosaurs may have occurred, enough survived the cosmic disaster to evolve into modern day birds.

****

The Black Mamba is native to Africa and is one of the most poisonous snakes in the world. But, don't spend your next safari looking for a black snake in the grass. The Black Mamba is actually light colored, ranging from tan to gray. It gets its name from the color of the inside of its mouth…which incidentally is the last thing you want to see!

****

I grew up in Oklahoma to the frequent sound of tornado sirens and my dad's midnight cries, "Get in the storm cellar." Years later the Air Force took me to North Florida where I became intimately familiar with hurricanes. Living in places prone to violent weather has a way of instilling the weather bug inside you, and my addiction to all things weather related has led me to accumulate more weather trivia and weather related anecdotes than my wife can bear.

So, now it's your turn to hear my weather stories.

I'll begin with a tornado. It was the night of the huge tornado outbreak in 1974. On April 3, 1974, a tornado measured at over one mile wide, with cloud tops above 60,000 feet (now considered an F5), ripped through Xenia, Ohio, knocking a train off its tracks and killing 34 people in this rural community.

I was in Oklahoma City that spring, and while we were not directly impacted by the 1974 Super Outbreak, every spring in Oklahoma brings the threat of tornadoes.

The initial storm rolled through our area and I remember coming out of the cellar to an eerie calm. Before the Internet and 24 hour cable news, the only way to find out what was going on in your community was to see it for yourself, so we loaded into the car and took off down Interstate 35.

I remember seeing a huge Kentucky Fried Chicken bucket crashed in the middle of the road, with over six feet of concrete encasing the base of the pole used to support the revolving bucket billboard tossed like a toothpick across the Interstate. Sadly, the bucket was not full of fried chicken, as my childhood imagination often pictured.

Hours later we returned home and noticed that in our haste to observe damage across town, we missed the damage to our own home. A six inch gap in the roof of our house connecting the garage to the kitchen area of our house was missing. While we our out snooping on other people's travails, our house had filled with ankle deep water.

As for hurricanes…

A tropical storm becomes a hurricane when its winds exceed 74 miles per hour. According to the Saffir-Simpson Scale, hurricanes are categorized from 1 to 5.

1. Category 1 Wind Speeds: 74-95 MPH
2. Category 2 Wind Speeds: 96-110 MPH
3. Category 3 Wind Speeds: 111-129 MPH
4. Category 4 Wind Speeds: 130-156 MPH
5. Category 5 Wind Speeds: 157+ MPH

During Hurricane Camille's Category 5 landfall in the Biloxi, Mississippi area in 1969, a 24 foot storm surge killed 15 people when it destroyed a church where residents were sheltering. Further north, the storm killed 153 in Virginia due to flooding.

On a personal level, I was living in a mobile home in the Florida Panhandle when Hurricane Opal came calling in 1995. When I contacted the landlord about any property protection issues he wished for me to be on the lookout for, he responded curtly, "Forget the trailer. Just get out."

I left within twenty minutes and spent the night on the road a hundred miles north in Alabama. Notably, Hurricane Opal made landfall as a Category 4 hurricane, with the lowest recorded barometric pressure for a hurricane that did not reach the Category 5 level.

****

The *Motown Sound* referred to popular music produced and recorded by artists under the Motown Record Corporation label in Motor City (Detroit) during the 1960s and 1970s. The Motown Record Corporation moved from Detroit to Los Angeles in 1972. Artists who recorded with Motown include: Marvin Gaye, Supremes, and the Temptations, among many others.

****

An ostrich is the largest living bird in the world. While it can't fly, it can run in short spurts at 45-60 miles per hour. It has a wingspan of 7 feet, and measured from the ground to their erect head, can stand 9 feet tall. Ostriches are recognized as the most dangerous birds on the planet, and use their powerful legs to break bones.

The Emu, which looks like a smaller version of an ostrich, is also dangerous, and prefers to rip the guts open of their victims.

Bottom Line: Ostriches and Emus may look cute, but watch out…they're also dangerous.

****

Have you ever referred to money as *dough* or *bread*? It's unclear when these slang words became popular, but the earliest print proof of the word *dough* in reference to money appeared in the mid 19th century. Lexicographers believe the words *bread* and *dough* suggest the importance of money in sustaining life.

****

The worst natural disaster to ever hit the planet was a 1931 flood in China that reportedly killed up to 4 million people. The Yangtze and Yellow Rivers run from west to east across the center of China, and every year floods from these rivers impact the lives of millions.

In 2012 China completed construction of the massive Three Gorges Dam across the Yangtze River, ranked as the largest hydroelectric dam in the world.

****

The Great Mississippi Flood of 1927 buried 27,000 square miles of the Mississippi Delta area under 30 feet of water and mud. The flood mainly impacted African-American farmers, and contributed to the mass migration out of the South and into the Upper Midwest.

****

One of the strangest slang words for money is the word *sawbuck*. A sawbuck is a ten dollar bill, and is believed to come from the x-shaped legs on a sawhorse. The X denotes the number 10 in Roman numerals. As for the word *buck*, that seems to relate to the trading of deer hides for currency.

Speaking of currency, the Austrian economist Ludwig Von Mises once stated, "Government is the only agency that can take a useful commodity like paper, slap some ink on it, and make it totally worthless." In an apparent reference to Nazism, he is also famous for stating, "To defeat the aggressors is not enough to make peace durable. The main thing is to discard the ideology that generates war."

Then again, as Mark Twain once snipped, "In all matters of opinion, our adversaries are insane."

****

Rankings of the richest people on the planet fluctuate, with people like Bill Gates, Larry Ellison, and Warren Buffett making the top 10 list year after year. Currently, Bill Gates is listed as the richest man alive with a reported net worth of $76 billion. Most billionaires' wealth is tied to their ownership of stock, thus their wealth moves up and down daily with the stock market.

****

Chocolate contains caffeine and theobromine, which acts as a stimulant. It also has a diuretic effect, which can send you packing off to the restroom.

****

Proctor & Gamble Company is an old American company, based in Cincinnati, Ohio. It is known for household name products like *Tide*, *Ivory Soap*, and *Crest* toothpaste. In 1863 James Gamble added air to his soap recipe by whipping the mixture. As it turns out, the air enriched bar of soap floated, and started a 100 plus year marketing campaign that has helped build one of the premiere companies in the world.

****

The Brits love their hot tea, and reportedly drink over 60 billion cups per year. With a population of just over 64 million, that equates to 93 cups per person; however, if you subtract the non-tea drinking infants, toddlers and alcohol drinkers from the equation, you just about get to my wife's average of 12 cups per day.

Here are some more interesting tea facts...

1. Tailings are considered the worst grade of tea, and are literally the parts of the tea plant swept up from the tea processing plant floors. Powdered teas are generally composed of tailings.
2. The Dutch East India Company was chartered in 1602 to import tea and spices from Asia to European markets.
3. The botanical name for tea plants is Camellia Sinesis.
4. There are four types of tea: white, green, oolong, black.
5. Tea works as appetite suppressant and can help you diet.

****

Ninja warriors are considered the first special forces type warriors in history. Their success, copied to this day by special forces units around the world, relied upon speed, aggression, and surprise. The only notable deviation from the original Ninja tactics currently being employed is the use of technology as a force multiplier.

****

The Heiligenstadt Testament is an 1828 document written by Ludwig van Beethoven where he is weighing suicide against the quest to finish his mission to share his music with the world. Fortunately for Ludwig and the world, he chose to continue composing music, despite being deaf.

****

When the notorious Bonnie and Clyde were gunned down by a posse in Louisiana on May 23, 1934, Bonnie Parker was only 23 years old. Her partner, Clyde Barrow, was 25. Bonnie and Clyde were bank robbers and murderers operating in the central part of the United States, primarily Texas, Oklahoma, and Louisiana. They are believed to have killed nine police officers, as well as several civilians.

Clyde Barrow's weapon of choice was a Browning Automatic Rifle (BAR). The BAR model M1918 used by Barrow fired a .30-06 bullet, and was designed especially for soldiers fighting in the trenches of World War I. It was lethal, and allowed Bonnie and Clyde to shoot their way out of numerous police ambushes.

****

The word *materiel*, spelled with an e, is the correct spelling of military equipment and supplies. It is typically pronounced, ma-tear-ee-el.

****

The *Commanding Heights* is an economics term first attributed to Lenin following the Bolshevik Revolution. In Lenin's time, the commanding heights of the Russian economy referred to key industries like transportation, energy, and agriculture. Lenin believed his control of these commanding heights gave him control of the entire economy, despite the continued existence of small business enterprises in early communist Russia. In today's economy, the areas of education and healthcare are deemed the commanding heights of our economy, suggesting a political motive behind the federal government's involvement in these sectors.

****

Clothing colors were once limited by the natural dyes that could be created from plants and shells. These colors tended to be muted and even drab. However, in 1856 a man named William Henry Perkin accidentally discovered synthetic colors when he was experimenting with a mixture of quinine. Since then, and much to the delight of fashionistas and kitchen remodelers worldwide, thousands of artificial colors have been created.

****

There are over 964 million websites online today; however, an estimated 75% of those sites are not active.

As for personal blogs, two new blogs go online every second around the world. It's unclear how many blogs go offline every second. Most blog readers are early risers, with most readers visiting their favorite sites around 8 a.m., presumably checking the status of their favorites before heading off to work or school.

The correct definition of a blog is a "weblog online diary."

****

The expression *Mad as a Hatter* was very accurate, as the mercury used by hat makers caused severe nerve damage—resulting in mental impairments.

****

A *haberdasher* is a person who sells sewing supplies, such as material, needles, and thread.

****

Shoeless Joe Jackson's real name was Joseph Jefferson Jackson. He batted left handed and threw right handed. He was 6'1" tall and weighed 200 pounds.

Shoeless Joe Jackson is best remembered as the man who fixed the 1919 World Series while playing for the Chicago Black Sox. However, in the Series he is accused of fixing, he batted .375, got 12 hits, and scored 5 runs.

****

Computers use the numbers 0 and 1 to denote a transistor setting of "off" and "on." Using a combination of these numbers is known as a binary number system. For example, the binary number 01 converts to the decimal value of 1, and the number 010 equals 2.

****

A *donkra* is a cross between a donkey and a zebra. Why anybody would bother breeding a donkey with a zebra remains a mystery.

****

Anybody that watches James Bond movies knows his favorite drink is a martini, "shaken, not stirred." However, the creator of the James Bond character, Ian Fleming, actually characterized Bond as a whiskey drinker.

Despite Fleming's fame for creating the James Bond 007 character, he also wrote children's books, such as the classic *Chitty-Chitty-Bang-Bang.*

****

J.R.R. Tolkien's *Lord of the Rings* was heavily influenced by his World War I experiences. The three volume set was originally published in 1954 and 1955.

****

A six-toed cat is known as a polydactyl, and is typically named something like *Big Foot*, or *Mitts*.

****

The most popular cat names include *Kitty, Oreo,* and *Tiger*. Among dog lovers, the most popular names include *Jack, Bear,* and *Rocky*. And in case you didn't know, the name *Gizmo* is quickly climbing the name popularity list for both cats and cute dogs with quirky personalities.

Naming a pet is serious business, and should always be left up to the children in the family. In my case, this has resulted in a string of pet names like *Bun-Bun, Blackjack, Sambam, Puddles,* and *Whizbang*.

Of all my pet names, *Puddles* was most aptly named for his uncanny ability to leave puddles on the living room floor, despite multiple daily walks and free access to the backyard.

Puddles had what the vet called a "nervous bladder," and despite never having been harmed by the UPS truck or its driver in any way, the mere sound of the big brown truck coming into the neighborhood sent him into a peeing frenzy. My wife suspects his fear of the UPS truck was related to her regular shipment of pet supplies and dog medicine that arrived via UPS. For his sake, and the comfort of others, I hope there are no UPS trucks in doggie heaven.

By the way...UPS stands for United Parcel Service. They deliver over 15 million packages to businesses and residents around the world, daily.

****

Terminal velocity is the highest speed a falling object can attain as it falls towards earth. Terminal velocity is limited by gravitational pull and the air resistance created by the size and shape of the object. A peregrine falcon is considered one of the fastest animals in the sky, and can dive at 242 miles per hour.

Some busy airports employ falcons to patrol the airspace and frighten other birds away, decreasing the likelihood of aircraft bird strikes.

****

Methuselah is the oldest person cited in the Holy Bible. He lived 969 years.

****

The Great Lakes are Huron, Ontario, Michigan, Erie, and Superior.

The acronym, HOMES, is the easiest way to remember the names of the Great Lakes.

One fifth of the world's freshwater is in the Great Lakes. The deepest of the five lakes is Superior, also known as an Inland Sea, with an average depth of 483 feet.

****

From Lookout Mountain near Chattanooga, Tennessee, you can see seven states: Tennessee, Kentucky, Virginia, South Carolina, North Carolina, Georgia and Alabama.

According to park officials, one of the most frequent questions asked by tourists gawking at the wooded horizon goes something like this: Where are the lines separating the states?

****

Over 80,000 miles of cable was used in the construction of the Golden Gate Bridge.

And just so you'll know, the Golden Gate Bridge is actually more orange colored than gold. The name pertains to San Francisco's role as the gateway to the goldfields and the golden state.

****

And speaking of bridges, the Mackinac Bridge in the Upper Peninsula of Michigan is 552 feet high and 26,372 feet long. The suspension bridge surface is made of expanded metal, which means drivers can see the water beneath them as they traverse the bridge.

Bridge officials routinely assist vertigo prone drivers by driving their cars across the bridge for them. The scientific name for the fear of bridges is *gephyrophobia*.

****

Barely outside the shadow of the Golden Gate Bridge is the island of Alcatraz, with its infamous federal prison by the same name. Alcatraz was closed in 1963.

****

In the David and Goliath story, Goliath was said to be nine and a half feet tall.

The average height of adult American males today is five feet ten inches. Interestingly, American soldiers in the Revolutionary War were on average three inches taller than their British counterparts.

****

The phrase "In God We Trust" first appeared on American coins in 1864.

****

Of all the classical and highly feared monsters you may have heard about, Big Foot is the only one who may have actually existed. The scientific name for Big Foot is *Gigantopithecus Blacki*.

****

Dinosaur fossils were once believed to be the remains of dragons, and were prized for their potential health and fertility properties.

****

Cryptozoology is the study of creatures that don't exist.

****

Not all cats hate water! The Turkish Van (from the shores of Lake Van in Turkey) loves water and will jump into the bathtub with you if you leave the bathroom door open.

****

The word *aloha* is a Hawaiian word for hello and goodbye. However, it also represents love and the Hawaiian way of life.

****

Maurice Sendak wrote and illustrated the classic children's book, *Where the Wild Things Are.* His original intent was to write and illustrate a book about horses, but to his horror, he discovered he could not draw horses, and chose instead to draw things that "looked just like his relatives."

Where the Wild Things Are was first published in 1963, and has remained a bestseller on sites like Amazon for years. At its release, it was the number one illustrated children's book of the year…which is pretty good for a guy who openly admits he cannot draw a horse.

****

Michelangelo's sculpture of *David* was carved from an enormous block of flawed marble which had set in the quarry, unwanted, for decades.

****

"Amber waves of grain" once referred to the swaying of tall stalks of wheat across our "fruited plain." However, the genetically modified wheat grown today focuses on the growth of the wheat kernel itself, reducing the stalk to a mere few inches in length.

And speaking of amber...

Amber is considered a semi-precious stone, but in fact, it is made from petrified tree resin. At one time during the Middle Ages, amber was considered more precious than gold, and warlords defended access to amber enriched beaches under their control to the death.

****

The expression "don't take any wooden nickels" is an American saying that advises people to be cautious in their business dealings. A wooden nickel is typically a wooden coin manufactured as a souvenir of an event, such as the 1933 Chicago World's Fair.

****

Alexander Graham Bell invented the telephone in 1876. Interestingly, his first paying customer was a hard sell, as the first customer noted he could talk to himself all day, without the benefit of a phone.

Decades later, the first fax machine salesmen faced the exact same resistance.

****

Celery was once considered a "rich man's" food. It was served in the middle of the table like a bouquet, with the leaves spread out like exotic flowers.

****

There are only two species of spiders harmful to humans in America: *Black Widow* and *Brown Recluse.*

Deaths by spider bites in North America are extremely rare, and are usually the result of toxic shock, or a weak immune system in its victim. That said, a Black Widow bite can be very painful and the subsequent symptoms may make you shout: "Just shoot me and get it over with."

As for the Brown Recluse, its necrotic venom rots flesh, and can leave you with golf ball size holes in the skin and tissue surrounding the bite area. Medical treatment is recommended for both of these spider bites.

****

There is a difference between poison and venom. Poison is a toxic substance that you ingest, whereas venom is a toxic substance received from a sting or bite from a venomous plant or animal.

****

Spider hunters once counted 842 spiders in a square meter of grass in England.

****

The Brazilian Wandering Spider is the deadliest spider in the world. The spider hangs out in the tropical forests of South and Central America. An effective anti-venom is available, but if you're bitten in a remote area where doctors are scarcer than horse feathers, you may be toast.

****

Spiders are not insects, they are arachnids. An insect has six legs; whereas an arachnid has eight legs.

****

The famous talking horse, *Mister Ed*, moved his lips for the camera because of the peanut butter applied to the inside of his lips.

Fortunately, horses love peanut butter, and are especially fond of peanut hay made from baling the stalks and leaves of peanut plants left over from harvesting the legumes.

From a farm kid's perspective, peanut hay was the worst. The bales are easily two to three times heavier than a normal bale of hay made from grass, and the stiff stalks can gouge your arms and stomach when you lift the bale onto the truck…hard work for peanuts in pay.

****

The average height of an adult male in Indonesia is five feet two inches.

****

Linguists estimate the Sami speaking people of Scandinavia have over 180 words for snow and ice, and as many as 300 different words to describe the different types of snow.

****

At minus 40 degrees Fahrenheit, unprotected skin will freeze in less than 5 minutes.

****

In the 1939 film classic, *The Wizard of Oz*, Buddy Ebsen was first selected to play the Tin Woodman. Unfortunately, it was quickly discovered Buddy was allergic to the silver paint he would have to wear to play the role. The role was given to Jack Haley…who did a great job.

Buddy Ebsen's real name was Christian Ludolf Ebsen, Jr. Most of us remember Buddy for his role as Jed Clampett in *The Beverly Hillbillies*.

****

The Pony Express carried letter mail and small packages on horseback from St. Joseph, Missouri to Sacramento, California for only 19 months, during the years 1860 and 1861. It was made obsolete by the arrival of telegraph lines.

The Pony Express used 120 riders and 400 horses to deliver mail within 10 days. Riders raced from station to station, exchanging horses and occasionally riders, at 157 stations staged 10 miles apart.

****

The creators of the Pony Express were deeply religious and required riders to swear an oath that they would not cuss, drink alcohol, or fight.

****

Mark Twain was a pen name for Samuel Clemens. He adopted the name from a Mississippi riverboat term meaning "two marks" on a rope that measured the depth of river water. Two marks equaled two fathoms, or about 12 feet.

****

Agastopia is a strange word that means the admiration of a specific body parts. For example, when a man says he is a 'leg man" that means he has an agastopia for legs.

****

A gabelle is a tax on salt. During the 1930 independence marches in India, Gandhi led a group of Indians to the sea to manufacture salt, thus nullifying the British tax on salt. At the time, the salt tax represented over 8 percent of tax revenues, which would be the equivalent of erasing the revenues garnered by county and state sales tax collection in America...a lot of money!

****

Lewis and Clark discovered many of the Mandan Indians in the Upper Midwest of America had blue eyes. At first, these early 19th century explorers attributed the blue eyes to French trappers and hunters in the area, but the Mandan's contested this, claiming they had always had blue eyes.

****

The expression *paying through the nose* comes from a tax the Danes imposed on Ireland in the 9th century. Apparently, a census was taken by counting noses, with taxes due for each nose counted. Refusal to pay the tax resulted in brutal punishment, including the removal of one's nose.

****

Sightings of the Loch Ness Monster, also known as *Nessie*, date back over 1,500 years.

****

A *ley line* is a natural or manmade geographical marker such as a mountain top, monument, or megalithic structure that aided cross-country travelers prior to the advent of marked roads and GPS navigation.

****

The Kensington Runestone was discovered in Minnesota in 1898. It is a large stone with writing on it that suggests Scandinavian explorers visited North America in the 14th century. Most scientists consider the stone a hoax; however, evidence of Icelandic and Norwegian fishermen fishing the Grand Banks area of Nova Scotia at the time suggests the European discovery of the Western Hemisphere may have pre-dated Columbus. Pictographs of tall ships sailing in the Great Lakes also suggest early explorers were in the area of Minnesota long before the western migration of European settlers several hundred years later.

****

1939 was a banner year for Hollywood, with movies like...

1. *The Wizard of Oz*
2. *Gone With the Wind*
3. *The Adventures of Huckleberry Finn*
4. *The Hound of the Baskervilles*
5. *The Hunchback of Notre Dame*
6. *Mr. Smith Goes to Washington*
7. *Stagecoach*

****

The story of a large whale that was known for destroying whaling ships was immortalized in the book *Moby Dick*, by Herman Melville. At the time Melville wrote his novel, there were reports of a whaling ship named Essex being sank by a whale.

****

In bible trivia, Jonah was reportedly swallowed by a great fish. While the story often depicts a whale swallowing Jonah, in actuality, a whale is a mammal, and not a fish. However, given that taxonomic classification was not popular at the time, it is easy to see how a whale may be called a large fish. For details on this story, see the book of Jonah.

****

After a 56 year trade and travel embargo with Cuba, the United States began to allow its citizens to travel to Cuba. On December 12, 2015, airline executives negotiated the rights to making up to 110 daily flights from the United States to Cuba.

The tourism infrastructure in Cuba is antiquated and unable to handle a massive influx of American tourism, creating a black market in the housing industry where people in Cuba can earn more by renting a room out for one night than they can earn working their state allocated job for a month.

Reportedly, European tourists who were never subjected to the American travel embargo were heard complaining in a Havana bar, "Well, the Americans are coming. There goes Cuba."

****

John Steinbeck won the Pulitzer Prize for his book, *The Grapes of Wrath,* in 1939. One year later the book was made into a movie, featuring Henry Fonda as Tom Joad. Ever the trouble maker, Tom is released from an Oklahoma prison in time to get home just as his family is packing for California. Once they arrive, Tom joins a group of labor agitators and makes life miserable for his mother, played by Jane Darwell.

The migrant worker camp portrayed in both the book and the movie remains operational to this day, and is located just south of Arvin, California.

Steinbeck lived much of his life in the Salinas and Monterey areas of California. Later, as a resident of New York City, he wrote a book called *Travels with Charley,* which was a travelogue of sorts, depicting his adventures travelling around America with his poodle.

At the end of the book Steinbeck tells the story of being frustrated to the point of tears as he attempted to find his way onto the George Washington Bridge. When a police officer asked him if he was okay, Steinbeck replied (and I'm paraphrasing here), "I've just travelled across the entire country, and now that I'm only a couple blocks from home, I'm lost."

****

In Catholicism, the Pope is protected by the Pontifical Swiss Guard. In 1506 a company of Swiss soldiers entered the Vatican and were blessed by Pope Julius II. At the time, the Swiss were known as mercenaries and courageous soldiers. Pope Julius II invited the Swiss Guard to become the *Defenders of the Church*.

Centuries later, one of the co-conspirators in the Lincoln Assassination, John Surratt, who was of Swiss ancestry, escaped North America and become a member of the Pontifical Swiss Guard.

****

Stop trying to sneak up on that housefly in order to swat it. A fly has a compound eye, made up of thousands of small lenses…which means they a virtual 360 degree view on their environment.

****

The old cowboy song, "Git along little dogies" is not a ballad about dogs. In cowboy lingo, a dogie is a steer.

****

According to veterinarians, the Bernese Mountain Dog has the shortest expected lifespan among dogs, at 7 years. The Chihuahua wins the prize for longevity, and will be chewing your furniture, digging holes in your backyard, and winning your heart for 20 years.

****

Can't stand vegetables? Did you know there is a scientific name for the fear of vegetables? It's lachanophobia. So, the next time you struggle to make up an excuse not to eat half cooked frozen peas or asparagus that tastes like a dirty cotton rope, just tell the cook you suffer from a rare disorder of lachanophobia. You'll be excused.

****

I have relatives in Oklahoma and Arkansas who refuse to come to California out of fear of earthquakes. Ironically, the New Madrid Fault Line along the Mississippi River in Missouri and Arkansas is home to one of the most powerful quakes to ever hit North America. And currently in Oklahoma, residents are experiencing dozens of earthquakes daily...possibly due to a change in oil extraction technologies that involve injecting high pressure water into the wells.

****

In 1811 and 1812, a series of earthquakes along the New Madrid Fault Line were powerful enough to reverse the flow of the Mississippi River. Madrid is not pronounced like the capital of Spain, but like this: Mad-drid.

****

In Alaska, the powerful earthquake to strike the Anchorage area on Good Friday in 1964 (March 27) was measured at 9.2. The shaking lasted for 4 minutes and 38 seconds.

As a teenager I often watched movies in the 4th Avenue Theater in downtown Anchorage. Immediately after entering the theater you have to take a flight of stairs down, as the entire theater dropped, intact, about ten feet during the quake. In photos of the earthquake, you can see the theater marquee level with the sidewalk.

****

Humans have about 5 million scent glands in his nose and sinuses. A dog, on the other hand, may have up to 300 million scent glands. Is it any wonder that a bloodhound can following an escaped prisoner across swamps and down paved roads?

****

When it comes to hearing, once again, your dog has you beat. Humans can hear sounds up to about 23,000 Hertz, but a dog can hear high pitched sounds up to 45,000 Hertz. Another advantage dogs have in the hearing department is their ability to shift their ears towards sounds.

****

Even a clock stuck flashing 12:00, 12:00, 12:00 day after day is right twice a day. Think about it. It's kind of like the blind squirrel who manages to stumble across just enough nuts to survive.

****

How long is a piece of string? Well, if you're talking about the largest ball of twine in the world, it would be approximately 1,600,000 feet long, or a little over 300 miles. This unusual tourist attraction is located in Cawker City, Kansas…which happens to be just down the road from the farm where Dorothy Gale lived with her Auntie Em.

****

Depending on humidity levels and barometric pressure, the speed of sound is approximately 768 miles per hour. Chuck Yeager broke the so-called *sound barrier* on October 14, 1947. Prior to becoming a test pilot with the U.S. Air Force, Yeager flew the P-51 Mustang in World War II. In 1944 he was shot down over France and escaped to Spain with the help of the French Resistance.

****

The notion that France surrendered to the Germans without a fight in World War II is a myth. In fact, 85,310 French soldiers died defending their homeland from the Nazi invasion, and 940,000 French soldiers spent the war in German POW camps.

****

1972 is a red later year in American history, with 54,589 traffic fatalities that year. Since then, the number has slowly declined as seatbelt laws and improved vehicle safety have decreased the number to a still tragic average of around 33,000 per year. This number translates to about 10 deaths per 100,000 people…less than half the death rate experienced in 1972.

****

Despite the political satire that suggests Al Gore invented the Internet, the actual backbone of the Internet began with the Department of Defense's Advance Research Projects Agency (ARPA). On December 5, 1969, ARPA linked its computers with computers from several universities, including the University of Utah and the University of California, Santa Barbara. The Internet was originally known as ARPANET.

****

Sputnik launched an international space race when the Soviet Union beat America to space with the first orbiting satellite. Sputnik was launched on October 4, 1957. Sputnik fell to earth and burned up in the atmosphere when it lost battery power on January 4, 1958…but its greatest success was in jumpstarting the American space program, leading to John F. Kennedy's famous speech on September 12, 1962 where he challenged Americans to commit to putting a man on the moon before the end of the decade.

****

The national average expenditure for students in Kindergarten through 12th grade is $10,608 per year. In New York, the average cost per student is $20,266 per year. Despite the highest student costs in the world, the U.S. ranks 14th in educational achievement.

****

A seismograph is used to detect and measure earthquakes. It is also capable of detecting and measuring the ignition of explosive devices, and has proven effective in deterring nuclear arms treaty violations among various nations.

****

A seismograph uses a scale known as the Richter Scale to measure the strength of an earthquake. The Richter Scale was created by two seismologists, Charles Richter and Beno Gutenberg, in 1935. Interestingly, the way the scale works, and earthquake measured 5 on the scale is 10 times more powerful than an earthquake with a measurement of 4.

****

A small earthquake is NOT a trembler. It is a temblor.

****

12 men have walked on the moon. Among them was Neil Armstrong, who was the first to walk on the moon on July 20, 1969. The last man to walk on the lunar surface was Eugene Cernan on December 14, 1972.

****

The prime meridian used for all international navigation and time keeping was established in Greenwich, England, in 1851. Several decades passed before France conceded to Greenwich, and not Paris, as the starting point for all longitudinal lines.

****

A prime number is any positive integer, other than 0 and 1, that can only be divided by itself and 1. For example, the number 3 is a prime number because it cannot be equally divided by anything other than itself and 1. Other notable primes include: 5,7,11,13,17,19,23.

****

The only even numbered prime number is 2, and no prime number greater than 5 can end with a 5. Any number, other than 0 and 1, that is not a prime number, is considered a composite number.

****

Central tendencies in statistics are measured and expressed using a *mean*, a *mode*, or a *median*.

The *mean* is a simple mathematical average of all the data points in question. For example, to find the average age of people attending a concert, you would simple add up the ages all the concert attendees, and then divide by the number of attendees.

Using the same example, a *mode* is simply the age of the concert attendees that occurs most frequently. For example, if 100 people were in attendance, and 42 of them were 23 years old, and no other age equaled or exceeded 42 incidences, the mode for this group would be 23.

Finally, the *median* is the number that sits in the middle. That is, if you ranked the ages of the concert attendees by age from youngest to oldest, the age where half are younger and half are older, would be the median.

Understanding the distinction between these three measurements of central tendency and how they are derived, is important, as statisticians can change the perception or characterization of the numbers by using a central tendency that can potentially distort or mislead readers.

For example, if the average age of concert attendees was skewed, or pulled in one direction by a handful of very elderly attendees, concert promoters may wish to avoid publishing the average age to avoid discouraging younger people from attending. Likewise, if an entire class of high school seniors attended the concert, the mode would be disproportionately swayed towards 17 or 18, even if the rest of the concert attendee population ranged in age from 60 to 90.

In that case, the average age of attendees may be in the 60s, but if the concert promoter published a mode of 17, he or she could dramatically change the perception of who attended the concert.

When you see central tendencies reported, always use critical thinking, and consider why one central tendency was chosen over another.

****

The caloric value in a serving of cooked rice can be reduced by as much as 60% by adding a few tablespoons of coconut oil to the water when boiling the rice. The rice should then be refrigerated for at least 12 hours before eating. If you plan ahead, this is a great way to enjoy rice without the typical caloric impact of this starchy grain.

****

The Los Angeles Unified School District is the second largest school district in America, with 1,087 schools and over 640,000 students ranging from Kindergarten through 12th grade. New York City has the largest school district in the nation, with over 1.1 million students.

****

A *Blue Moon* is not blue. In fact, it looks just like any other full moon. The term Blue Moon is the name given a second full moon in the same calendar month. Since this is a rare occurrence, the expression, "once in a Blue Moon," means, "not very often."

As for the various colors of the moon, changes in the visible appearance of the moon are a result of the local atmospheric conditions impacting the air around the viewer. For example, a forest fire in the mountains east of your location can make a rising full moon appear red.

****

A *liquid* asset is anything of monetary value that can be immediately converted into cash. For example, a stock actively traded on the New York Stock Exchange may be considered liquid because it can be sold and turned into cash…usually the same day. An *illiquid* asset is something like your house. It's worth money (hopefully more than the mortgage due), but it may take several months to sell and convert into cash in your pocket.

****

Ninja warriors depend upon stealth to complete their night missions. As a rule, Ninjas never attack eight days before or after a full moon.

****

Speaking of moons, a *Harvest Moon* is a full moon in late summer to early fall. It earned this name by giving extra light to allow field workers to bring in the crop long after sunset. A full moon around Halloween is traditionally called a Harvest Moon.

****

The term *Gibbous Moon* refers to a phase of the moon when it is more than half full. A *waxing* moon is increasing towards fullness, and a *waning* moon is decreasing towards a new moon.

****

The Bay of Fundy north of Maine and on the southern edge of Nova Scotia has the highest tidal range in the world. Tides in this area can range by as much as 53 feet from high tide to low tide.

****

Honey is believed to have an indefinite shelf life, with honey recovered from Egyptian pyramids remaining edible after thousands of years of storage. The low water content and high sugar content of honey naturally kills bacteria.

****

The U.S. Air Force pays Northrop Grumman $2 billion for each B-2 Stealth Bomber. To put this in perspective, a person earning $50,000 per year would have to work 40,000 years to pay for one plane. Based on America's population of 320 million, each citizen must contribute $6.25 in taxes to pay for one bomber.

During the initial test flights of the aircraft, it was discovered the aircraft's high tech radar could not distinguish a cloud from a mountain. Given this limitation, the aircraft was unable to fly on cloudy days.

****

When it comes to dump trucks, size matters. The world's largest dump trucks are used in open pit mining operations, such as the borax mine in Boron, California. The dump trucks used to haul material out of these pits are manufactured by Caterpillar. The body of the truck reaches above 51 feet, its tires stand over 13 feet tall, and the cargo hold is capable of carrying over 360 tons.

****

The next time you flush your toilet or drain your bathtub, pay attention to the direction the water swirls as it goes down the drain. In earth's northern hemisphere, water spins counter-clockwise. On the southern hemisphere, water spins clockwise. This phenomenon is known as the *Coriolis Effect*.

****

The United States Declaration of Independence was first signed by John Hancock, whose large signature at the bottom middle portion of the document became synonymous with the word signature, as in, "put your John Hancock on the dotted line." As he signed the document, Hancock stated, "I'm going to make my name so big, Ole King George will not have any problem finding it."

A common mistake is to ask people to place their *John Henry* on the dotted line. But John Henry was not one of the Founding Fathers. He was a legendary railroad builder in West Virginia who famously challenged a steam drill to a tunnel drilling race.

****

It's said that God created man, but it took Sam Colt to make them equal.

This expression comes from the role the Colt .45 revolver, also known as the *Peacemaker* or the *Great Equalizer*, played in the settling of the American West. It was invented in 1836 and its interchangeable parts, ease of use, and low cost due to its assembly line production made it the most popular firearm of its time.

But truth be known, the real equalizer in the American Wild West was the shotgun. For example, the gunfight at the O.K. Corral on October 26, 1881, was fought using Colt revolvers…with the exception of one shotgun. A dentist, professional gambler, and gunfighter named Doc Holliday selected a shotgun as his weapon of choice. During the gunfight, approximately 30 rounds were fired in rapid succession, with the majority of fired rounds missing their targets. Three of the nine gunfighters died in the fight, with Doc Holliday's shotgun doing the bulk of the damage.

****

Boot Hill was a common name for cemeteries in the American Wild West and is often associated with the final resting place for men who "died with their boots on." Typically, dying with your boots on referred to having a violent death, as opposed to dying of natural causes.

****

Have you ever yelled, "I got shotgun," when climbing into the front right seat of a car? The expression "riding shotgun" was first coined in 1919; however, it is typically associated with the position of an armed guard that rode next to the driver of a vehicle…such as a stagecoach.

The most popular firearm used by stagecoach guards was the Coach gun, which is a short-barreled shotgun, ideally suited for rapid movement and *scatter blast* effect.

****

With 7.3 billion people on Earth, is it any wonder there are oddball fun facts to share and enjoy?

There is a 20th century saying that originated in England, and not ancient China as some believe, that goes something like this: "May you live in interesting times." We do! We live in a fascinating, wonderful, and weird world. So, scroll down to check out what your friends, neighbors, and Darwin Award winning fools are plotting next.

****

Be on the lookout for killer technology!
According to scientists speaking to uber-elites at the 2016 Davos Conference in Switzerland, robotic technology and artificial intelligence is setting the stage for entire battles fought between warring machines…and the inevitable end result is that these same machines will then turn their weaponry against their human creators.
This exact scenario is what inspired Isaac Asimov to write about robot rules in his science fiction classic, *I, Robot*.

Asimov created the *Three Laws of Robotics*, which governed all robot behavior. These three rules essentially commanded robots to never harm humans, obey human commands, and protect itself, so long as the robot's self-protection does not violate the first two rules.

****

Charles Darwin was big on evolution and the survival of the fittest. But, did you know there was a prize for stupidity?

Trust me, you don't want this award, as you have to remove yourself from the gene pool (die) to qualify.

For example, Gene Harding of Springfield, Illinois (name and location changed to protect his family's privacy) failed to heed the warning on a motorcycle commercial featuring a man jumping his bike into the bed of a moving pickup truck.

Not to be outdone by a television stunt, Gene enlisted two friends to help him: one to drive the truck, and one to film it. Two seconds into the stunt Gene's motorcycle landed in front of the truck, where he promptly crashed and was tragically run over by his well-meaning friend.

Statistically, accidents are one of the top five causes of death in America. In 2013, 130,557 Americans died in accidents.

****

A 747 transport plane was forced to make an emergency landing when gas from the digestive tracts of over 2,000 goats in the cargo hold set off the fire alarms.

This whole smelly situation reminds me of my dearly departed nana, who always said, "If goats were meant to fly, God would have given them wings."

****

And speaking of flying, a Delta airlines flight recently permitted a *comfort turkey* to ride in the passenger cabin, seated in its own seat, next to its anxious master.

Apparently, a note from a doctor certifying you suffer from anxiety is all it takes to qualify for a comfort animal, and the Americans with Disabilities Act authorizes your use of a comfort animal in places where critters are normally prohibited.

****

The Pit Bull dog was once called a *Nanny* dog because they were good with children and fiercely protective of their human family.

Known for their strong bite, the Pit Bull exerts over 300 pounds per square inch when it clenches its jaws, and pound for pound, are considered the strongest breed of dog.

Sadly, due to misguided training, uncontrolled breeding, and irresponsible owners, the Pit Bull has gained a reputation for being untrustworthy and dangerous.

Despite their rep, Pit Bulls are used as therapy dogs, as search and rescue dogs, and narcotic and bomb sniffing. One Pit Bull, named Popsicle, sniffed out 3,000 pounds of cocaine in Hildago, Texas.

And by the way, the three headed dog named *Fluffy* in the *Harry Potter* stories, was modelled after a Pit Bull, and the *Little Rascals* sidekick was a Pit Bull named *Pete the Pup*.

One final note: Pit Bulls score an 83.4% passing rate on the American Temperament Test Society's exam…higher than the vaunted Border Collie, and only one notch below the American favorite, the Labrador Retriever.

****

The United Nations is always in search of new and innovative ways to feed the world's hungry. But their latest idea fails to meet my personal taste test.

Like Marie Antoinette advising the starving masses of 18th century France to eat cake, the experts at the United Nations have told the starving huddled masses of Africa to eat crickets.

As it turns out, a 100 gram bowl of crickets contains 12.9 grams of protein, 5 grams of fat, and 5 grams of carbohydrate. Dried and ground into flour, cricket flour can theoretically feed the world...so if you have any recipe ideas, I'm sure the U.N. would be happy to review them.

And in case you're interested, a 100 gram serving of grasshoppers contains 20 grams of protein, 6 grams of fat, and 4 grams of carbohydrate.

Now, I can hear it already...you're on a low carbohydrate diet.

Okay, try a giant water beetle. They pack a hefty 20 grams of protein per 100 grams of bug, and only have 2 carbohydrates per serving.

****

The feed to meat ratio farmers use to measure how much feed is required to produce a given amount of meat is critical to their profit margins, and is used extensively in agriculture to forecast the cost of raising a hog or steer to a marketable weight. Ironically, the feed to meat ratio for edible insects is 400 times greater than what is obtained in the traditional meat producing livestock.

So, the question remains: Do you have any good cricket or grasshopper recipes?

****

Sergeant Stubby, a Boston Bull Terrier, was the only war dog officially given a military rank. He was even issued a ration card, and was authorized three bones per day from the enlisted mess. Stubby served in the trenches of World War I, and was wounded three times by grenade and once by gunshot in the 17 battles he served in.

Stubby knew the sound of incoming gas canisters and saved his Army battle buddies on numerous occasions by sounding the alarm, and even alerted soldiers to a German spy. Sergeant Stubby is in the Smithsonian, and is displayed with a vest shrouded in campaign medals and multiple purple hearts.

Stubby was originally a stray that wandered into an Army camp. When the unit deployed, soldiers snuck Stubby aboard their ship. When faced with possible execution as a stow-away, Stubby performed a series of tricks, such as standing at attention and saluting, to prove he was a well-trained soldier, ready for action on the Western Front.

Not to be outdone, the Marines also had a Bull Dog in their midst, but according to reports, his only claim to fame was that he had a cute hat.

****

On July 15, 1974, a Florida news reporter named Christine Chubbuck committed suicide on live television by shooting herself.

Nationwide, the Center for Disease Control reports 41,149 people committed suicide in 2013. 50% of those deaths were caused by firearms, followed by suffocation and poisoning.

****

Sometimes, fact is stranger than fiction.

Back in 1975, the movie *Jaws* prompted many of us to give up on any ideas of swimming in the ocean. The story featured a 20 foot Great White shark as the villain eating hapless swimmers off the coast of a small New England town.

On January 18, 2016, a shark patrol spotted a Great White near a beach in Adelaide, Australia. The experts estimated its size at 23 feet...which is bigger than a stretch limousine, or your father's Buick.

****

The famed oceanographer, Jacques Cousteau, once stated, "When man enters the water, he enters the food chain...and he is not at the top."

Something to think about.

****

It's decided…Sandy Island does not exist.

For over 200 years a South Pacific island documented on every nautical map in existence, including Google Maps and Yahoo Maps, eluded further exploration.

As it turns out, researchers from Australia traced the source of the island's discovery, and found the original whalers on the ship *Velocity*, mistook a low lying reef for an island. For now, there is no evidence to suggest the island ever existed.

****

Area 51 is a secretive U.S. Air Force base located in the southwestern corner of Nevada. While the Air Force cannot deny the base is used to test new technologies, it remains mute when asked if the base is also used to house crashed UFOs.

The movie, *Independence Day*, released in 1996 and starring Will Smith, portrays Area 51 as a research facility where alien spaceships are being reverse engineered.

A Nevada state highway near Area 51 is called the Extra-Terrestrial Highway.

****

Thanks to the Mars Rover and Mars Observer missions, thousands of photos of the Mars' surface have become available to the public. Sharp-eyed enthusiasts have spotted rock formations that have a remarkable resemblance to earth creatures and formations. For example, here are just a handful of the notable finds: a mouse, lizard, godlike face, bear cub, spoon, woman spirit, crashed spaceship, Mars Stonehenge, and a gorilla and camel face-off.

The Mars Rover missions are robots, named *Spirit, Opportunity*, and *Curiosity*.

****

Where and how did the word *trivia* come from?

The word *trivia* is the combination of two Latin words, *tri* and *via*. It literally means three ways, or three roads, and comes from a tradition of posting greetings and announcements to travelers at an important intersection outside Rome.

It also has a more morbid source, and relates to a Roman law that required dead bodies to be buried outside the city limits. As a result, headstones for makeshift graves lined both sides of the roads leaving Rome. These headstones typically included carved endearments, such as, "we'll miss you," and "we will always remember you."

Travelers often passed the time reading headstones as they entered or left Rome, leading to a tradition of posting advertisements and announcements on the headstones.

****

During World War II, Army nurses used the acronym PWOP to describe being *pregnant without permission*. Unwed service women were discharged from service when found in PWOP status.

****

Speaking of nurses, the U.S. military recruited 74,500 nurses during World War II. Of those, 200 were killed in action.

****

Have you ever noticed when you're looking for a lost set of keys or your purse, you find the errant item(s) in the last place you look?

This phenomenon seems universal, but hides a simple truth…most of us stop the search when we find the lost item, therefore its hidden location is *always*, the last place we look.

****

A baby zebra must quickly learn the stripe pattern of his mother, or face a short life of hopeless searching in a sea of likeness.

****

I've found from countless do-it-yourself home projects, that any repair job requires at least three trips to the hardware store.

I love hardware stores, so this was never a problem...until my wife talked me into buying a house 22 miles outside town.

****

Most life forms on earth have iron-based blood, which accounts for the red color of oxygenated blood. Octopus and squid are different, and have blue blood, based on copper.

Can anyone say *alien*?

****

In England, girls call their bangs, *fringe*, and their braids, *plaits*. Then again, they also call cigarettes *fags*...a derogative word that can get you into a lot of trouble in America.

Charles Darwin once believed earthworms were extremely intelligent, and he even set up an elaborate earthworm farm to prove his hypothesis.

Fortunately, for all the bait fishermen and worm eating birds out there, he was proven wrong.

****

The bestselling Mary Kay lipstick is called, *Berry Kiss.*

****

I recently complimented my little nephew by claiming he was the best thing to come around *since sliced bread.*

To my surprise, he asked the simple question many of us never think to ask…

When was slice bread invented?

It turns out, the first *loaf at a time* bread slicer, which made the commercial production of sliced bread possible, was invented by a guy named Otto Frederick Rohwedder in 1928.

****

Have you ever met a cute little baby beluga whale?

If not, you're lucky. It turns out belugas are the smelliest animals on the planet…making the dreaded scent of a skunk smell downright rosy.

****

What does the wedding ring symbolize?

In ancient times, perhaps not too long ago, the ring became symbolic of the shackles and chains men used to restrain their captured wife as she adjusted to life away from her home or native village.

Somewhat associated with this act of capturing was the role of the best man, whose job it was to assist the love stricken groom-to-be in kidnapping his prospective wife. Presumably, the best man had to be good with a sword and a steadfast friend of the broom.

In the modern context, the wedding ring is symbolic of everlasting love, as its shape implies infinity. It's also useful for telling other suitors, "he's taken."

****

Not all brides of the world wear white (symbolizing purity), and instead simply wear their best dress. In contrast, brides in China prefer red gowns, as the color red is symbolic of good fortune and joy.

In America, there are over 2.1 million weddings each year. Sadly, there are approximately 900,000 divorces per year, and around 35,000 annulments.

****

Texas Tech University, located in Lubbock, Texas, has a student population of 35,893.

But this isn't about student enrollment. It's about me and my appreciation for what many authorities have claimed is the most beautiful student body in the country.

My wife attended Texas Tech, and since we only had one car capable of making it out of the driveway, I routinely picked her up after class. I didn't mind. In fact, I often showed up early, just to people watch.

Eventually, my wife caught on to my voyeuristic habit when I forgot to remove the baby car seat from the trunk where I had hidden it from view.

Like the wedding ring, nothing says "he's taken" like a baby car seat.

****

The Battle of Gettysburg during the American Civil War turned into a series of bloody skirmishes for high ground between the North and the South, leading to one of the deadliest confrontations of the war at Little Round Top.

The 20th of Maine Infantry Regiment, led by Colonel Joshua L. Chamberlain, found themselves out of position at the onset of battle and conducted an all-day forced march to reach Little Round Top in time to engage the enemy and defend the high ground. En route, Chamberlain found himself confused by a fork in the road.

Multiple witnesses in the unit later testified to the Secretary of War that an apparition appeared on horseback, pointing the way to the battlefield.

According to Chamberlain and his men, the ghost looked just like General George Washington.

Credited for valor and courage, the 20th of Maine's bayonet charge into Rebel positions was actually a necessity, as they had run out of ammunition and resorted to the bayonet charge in an act of inspired desperation.

Long after the Battle of Gettysburg, Chamberlain and his men remembered a silent ghost on horseback pointing the way to the battlefield that saved the day…and perhaps the Union.

****

Approximately 1.2 million Americans have died in wars from the Revolutionary War to the current conflicts in the Middle East and Afghanistan. 620,000 of those deaths are attributed to the Civil War.

****

Do birds fart?

Fortunately not, or we would all be in trouble. Could you imagine a world where flocks of pigeons pranced around cathedral steps farting? Or dodging waves of migrating ducks and geese as they crop dusted entire communities at will?

****

The shell of an ostrich egg is useful for carrying water in Africa.

****

What does it mean when somebody tells you, *Don't drink the Kool-Aid*?

Kool-Aid is a registered trademark of KraftFoods, Inc., and in this case is the unfortunate recipient of a horrible episode in American history.

In November 1978, 913 members of a cult group led by Jim Jones drank grape flavored water laced with cyanide and died, in the belief the end times were upon us.

So, when somebody says "don't drink the Kool-Aid," what they are really saying is, "don't be gullible," and be careful not to accept what you are being told as the truth.

****

How many vertebrae are in the long neck of a giraffe?

No more than usual, as it turns out. Despite being long, the giraffe's neck vertebrae are simply larger than other vertebrates, and not more numerous.

In case you're wondering, a giraffe has 7 neck vertebrae…the same number found in humans.

****

What if dogs could talk?

Well, for starts I would be in trouble, because like most dog lovers, I have shared many of my deepest secrets with my dogs. But why, among all the animals, are humans the only ones given the gift of speech?

First, it can be argued that all animals communicate, in one form or another, with their peers. But, the complexity of human speech is unique to humans.

Why? When I asked my wife this question she immediately knew the obvious answer: Speech was developed so mother-in-laws could remind men of their shortcomings.

Human speech is made possible by air from our lungs passing over the vocal chords (or folds) in our larynx. Male vocal chords are usually 17 to 25 millimeters in length; whereas female vocal chords are around 12 to 17 millimeters in length.

****

And speaking of millimeters…

A millimeter is one thousandth of a meter. For my American readers, a meter is about 39 inches, and a kilometer, or one thousand meters, is about 6 tenths of a mile.

To convert kilometers to miles in your head, simply multiply the first number in the kilometers given by six. For example, if a road sign says it 80 kilometers to Timbuktu, you would first ask yourself why you are on a road to Timbuktu, and then you would multiply the 8 by 6 to get 48. So, if I remember my times tables correctly, 80 kilometers equals approximately 48 miles.

If you come across a number like 89, you may want to round up to 90 and multiply 9 by 6 to get a more accurate conversion. If you have a calculator handy, you can multiply the exact number in kilometers by .62. So 89 kilometers times .62 equals 55 miles...but please, no texting or calculating while driving, because you see...

****

In America, texting while driving is now being considered as dangerous as driving under the influence.

The National Highway and Traffic Safety Administration compiles statistics relevant to *distracted driving*. Approximately 9 people die each day in America from distracted driving, and around 1,200 people are injured. Annually, this equates to 3,285 lives loss due to pesky text messages, stubborn hamburger wrappers, and dropped cigarettes.

All of which reminds me of the time a couple years ago when I took my eyes off the road for about half a second to count the change in my cup holder and found myself in the exit lane on a lonely stretch of I-40 somewhere near Tucumcari, New Mexico. As it turned out, the on ramp to get back on the interstate required backtracking four miles on a frontage road.

****

Pope Francis once worked as a bouncer in a bar in Argentina before becoming a Jesuit.

****

What if 9-1-1 did not exist?

Imagine a world where 9-1-1 did not exist. In the case of an emergency, you would be stuck finding the phonebook (if you even have one) and looking up the number for your local police, fire, or ambulance service.

The first 9-1-1 service started in 1968, and calls were directed to AT&T operators. Since then the service has expanded across the country to over 5,899 call centers. According to the National Emergency Number Association, Americans make over 240 million 9-1-1 calls per year, or on average 111 calls per day to each call center.

By the way…in most countries outside the U.S., the number for emergency calls is 9-9-9. When the American system was first set up, it made sense to use the number 9-1-1 because of AT&T's history of using the three digit number ending in 11 for information and operator assistance. For example, 4-1-1 gives you directory assistance, and 3-1-1 is used for non-emergency assistance with community issues.

****

Why is there an island just a stone's throw from downtown Manhattan that is totally uninhabited?

North Brother Island, in New York City was once a sanctuary, or prison, for people with infectious diseases. It wasn't a leper's colony, and once contained a huge hospital, that is now an empty and haunting brick building overgrown with trees, weeds, and brush.

The island is famous for housing Typhoid Mary…a former servant and cook in New York City who carried the dreaded disease, typhoid. After being banned from working around people, she refused to stop working in food service, and was eventually sent to North Brother Island to staunch the rapid spread of the disease.

Mary Typhoid Mallon died on North Brother Island in 1938. The island's hospital facility closed in the early 1960s, and the entire island is now considered a bird sanctuary.

Tragically, on June 15, 1904, a steamship called the General Slocum caught fire on the island's coast, killing over 1,000 people.

****

Have you ever stared up and wondered, "Why is the sky blue?"

Well, it's not always blue, as local weather conditions can change the color of the sky. There is an old saying that advises people to run for cover if they see a green sky, as it portends a tornado. In fact, a green sky does suggest a tornado is imminent because it is associated with the refraction of light from hail stones and severe thunderstorms.

The color green may also be associated with the presence of methane in the atmosphere in the early formation of the planet, which eventually gave wave to a oxygen and nitrogen rich atmosphere.

As far as the sky being blue, what we see is the result of light shining through the atmosphere, which acts like a prism. Molecules that reflect blue light are predominant in the sky.

And in case you're wondering, the air we breathe is 78% nitrogen and 21% oxygen. It's a delicate balance, where even a small tick upward in the oxygen levels could ignite the entire world's atmosphere like a bomb; give it a small tick downward and we'd all be rushing for our neighbor's scuba diving tanks.

****

A shark's egg sack is known by sailors as a *Mermaid's Purse*.

You can imagine the attraction sailors had for the legend of mermaids. Think about it, you're on a ship at sea with a hundred or more other guys, there is no Internet or cable television. You can't bring your girlfriend onboard to go whaling or exploring because women on a ship were considered bad luck, and nobody really understood anything about the briny deep.

Given those limitations to diversion, sailors naturally conjured images of the female form in everything they saw…including narwhales whose horn led sailors to believe they were *unicorns of the sea.*

****

What if a school of fish fell from the sky and landed on your front yard?

Sounds crazy, right? But it does happen occasionally in places like Florida where water spouts suck fish and frogs and other marine life forms into its vortex, spitting them out seconds later.

There have also been reported cases of frozen frogs dropping like hailstones, presumably victims of water spouts or tornadoes, which suck the doomed animals to high altitudes, where the animals freeze, and then drop like rocks.

****

The word *gollum* is an ancient word from Jewish tradition that meant monster, or night creature that steals your soul. It especially likes to prey on children.

Gollums reportedly visit you at night and sit on your chest...sometimes taking unspeakable liberties with their victims.

Incidentally, J.R.R. Tolkien borrowed the ancient legend of gollums to create his main villain in his book, *The Hobbit*.

****

Rumors that an 800 year old cell phone was found in an archeological dig in Austria have been proven false. The alleged *alien cell phone* turned out to be a cleverly disguised sculpture carved around the year 2013…and not during the waning years of the Roman Empire.

****

At its height, the Roman Empire ruled over 20% of the entire world's population. The official date of the empire's collapse in the west is generally accepted as 476 A.D. In the east, the Roman Empire continued to exist as what we now call the Byzantine Empire, based in Constantinople. The eastern faction of the Roman Empire collapsed in 1453 A.D.

****

Political correctness is a much maligned concept of not using hateful or discriminatory language towards people with disabilities or disadvantages. For example, referring to a person with a developmental disability as a retard is offensive and politically incorrect.

Taken to its extreme, using politically correct language effectively hides or avoids sensitive issues that may otherwise be confronted and resolved if clearly enunciated.

****

There is a rule of thumb among some medical doctors that states, if a pregnant woman can remain standing while she is having contractions, she is not dilated.

Okay, by now every mother reading this is probably wondering, that had to be a man who thought up that wacky idea. And I sympathize.

When my wife was pregnant with our first, she was reading a book on what to expect with her pregnancy and delivery. I was sitting on the couch reading a Louis L'Amour novel when suddenly this thick hardcover book went sailing over my head and crashed into the wall behind me.

According to my wife, the author claimed labor pains were nothing more than moderate to severe menstrual cramps.

Sometimes, a woman has to say, "enough is enough."

****

Where did the name America come from?

In 1507 a mapmaker named Martin Waldseemuller published a map of South America. He named the continent *America* after the explorer Amerigo Vespucci.

****

John Wesley Powell led a team of explorers down the Colorado River in 1869 and became the first known European/American to travel the length of the Grand Canyon on water.

Two members of his team left the party halfway down the gorge, convinced they were on a suicide mission, at best. The two men attempted to climb out of the canyon, and were never heard from again.

Days later the team emerged from the canyon into an area now known as Powell Lake.

****

The moon does not create light. Instead, it merely reflects light from the sun. It takes just over one second for the moon's light to reach earth.

****

Among the superstitious, it is considered bad luck to climb out of bed backwards.

Personally, I can attest to this, as the last time I tried it, I tripped over a corner of my bedspread and nearly gave myself a concussion. Simply put, it's always best to look where you're going—even if you're not superstitious.

****

Speaking of bad luck, the black cat has been maligned as a portent of ill fortune for centuries.

It's believed the troubles for black cats began in the 14th century, when victims of the devastating plague around 1348 blamed cats for bringing the evil plague upon them.

Ironically, as was later discovered, the Black Death was transmitted by fleas hitchhiking across Europe on the backs of rats. As the cat population in Europe was nearly decimated, the rat population surged…amplifying the impact of the plague.

****

The French folk singer, Edith Piaf, earned the nickname, *the little black sparrow*, because of her habit of wearing a little black dress during her performances.

The little black dress was first designed by another French singer and fashion designer, Coco Chanel. Coco's real first name was Gabrielle, but everybody called her Coco because of a song she frequently performed as a teenager about a bird that repeatedly chirped, *coco, coco*.

Interestingly, Coco's innovative designs led to major shifts in how women dressed, with an emphasis on allowing women to dress comfortably, and in many cases used the same materials and cuts popular with men's wear.

****

Culottes are a popular pants/dress in modern times, but they actually had there start in the Middle Ages…and were worn only by upper class men.

During the French Revolution (1789-1799), revolutionaries were known as *sans culottes*, meaning without culottes, in their attempt to separate themselves from the aristocratic classes, who at the time were losing their heads on yet another French favorite—the guillotine.

****

The *guillotine* is a mechanical device used to lop off the heads of its victims. Similar devices were in use prior to the French Revolution; however, in 1789, Dr. Joseph-Ignace Guillotin suggested the device be used as a humane method of executing members of the French aristocracy.

The device caught on, and was used in France until 1977.

****

I recently volunteered to help my wife wash the dishes after learning that no sane woman has ever murdered her husband while his hands were covered in dishwashing soap.

Makes sense! A sane woman would wait until he finished the dishes before pulling the trigger.

****

On October 18, 1867, Secretary of State William Seward authorized the U.S. purchase of Alaska from Russia. The price: $7 million, or around 2 cents per acre.

At the time, the public was highly critical of the purchase, and called it "Seward's Foley."

****

Bald eagles are not bald. In fact, their heads are covered with a thick layer of white feathers.

When the bald eagle was named, the word *bald* meant, white. As far as the bald eagle being selected as our national symbol, that happened on June 20, 1782 when the Great Seal of the United States was authorized.

At the time, Benjamin Franklin opposed the selection of the bald eagel as our national emblem, and instead wanted the wild turkey to receive that honor.

****

Humpback whales migrate from Alaska to Hawaii, preferring to spend their winters in the warm tropics, and summers in Alaska.

The only time of year humpback whales eat is during the few months they spend in Alaska, where they fatten up on tons of krill.

****

In June, 1999, the famous and bestselling horror novelist, Stephen King, was struck and critically injured by a van while taking a walk near his rural home.

According to King, the pain associated with his recovery exceeded anything he ever imagined in his stories.

****

In ranch country, it is considered a common courtesy to leave a gate like you found it. That is, if you open a gate, close it, and of you find a gate left open, chances are it was left open for a reason.

****

Why is a *Baker's Dozen* 13, and not 12?

Years ago, especially in Medieval Europe, a baker could be severely punished for shorting a customer. Traditionally, customers buy things like bagels, croissants, and now donuts, in units of a dozen. To reduce the risk of accidentally miscounting and giving the customer 11 rather than 12 bagels or croissants, bakers added an extra piece of bread.

In a modern bakery, a baker may offer a *Baker's Dozen* as a free bonus or customer goodwill promotion.

****

Carpet installers measure carpet in square yards, not square feet. We all know there are three feet in a yard; however, when converting the square footage of your home into square yards, be sure to divide by 9, and not 3, as there are 9 square feet in each square yard.

****

How many square feet are in an acre?

An acre of land contains 43,560 square feet.

I was recently looking at vacant home lots and noticed the sale sign was making a big deal about the "low-low price" of just $2 per square foot. Sounds good, right? Well, when you consider the converted ranch land had recently sold for $1,100 per acre, the square foot price put the per acre value at over $87,000...quite a markup for a few survey sticks and a poorly plowed dirt access road.

****

Ever heard the expression, *knock on wood*?

Around 200 A.D. a religious group in England and Gaul (France) known as the Druids, worshipped trees. They especially loved oak trees and believed these trees were inhabited with tree spirits. Druids tapped on trees to wake the spirits inside, to presumably ask for favors or blessings.

In a modern context, the expression, *knock on wood*, means to hope for good luck...or prevent ill fortune.

****

What is an *algae bloom*?

An algae bloom is a spike in the growth of algae in a specific body of water. These spikes are generally the result of unseasonably warm water, and the influx of chemicals and fertilizers into the water from ground erosion and runoff.

In 2015, the coast of China was hit by the largest ever recorded algae bloom, with over 11,000 square miles of beaches and waterways covered in a foot thick coat of green algae. In one city alone, government officials used bulldozers to remove 7,000 tons of algae from the beach.

****

What is a staurolite?

A staurolite is a crystal that naturally forms in the shape of a cross. According to legend, staurolites were created when the angels cried at Christ's crucifixion. Wherever the angels' tears fell, staurolites were created.

Always on the hunt for inspiration, Thomas Edison reportedly carried a staurolite in his pocket.

****

Of all the planets in our solar system, Jupiter reigns supreme. It is called the *King of Worlds*, and is larger than all the other planets…combined.

****

The Amazon River in South America is the longest river in the world, at 4,345 miles. At the point where the Amazon dumps into the Atlantic Ocean, its delta is over 150 miles wide, and its main central channel is 50 miles wide.

****

The most venomous spider in the world is the *Brazilian Wandering Spider*. To add insult to injury, this spider is big, and typically grows to over 6 inches (about the size of an adult hand) in width. Fortunately, this spider likes to conserve its venom, and rarely injects a lethal dose into its human victims.

Creepiest of all, the Brazilian Wandering Spider loves to hide in shoes!

****

Every mom knows one of the best ways to give your kid vitamin C is to toss an orange into their lunch bag. But did you know foods like chili peppers, kale, cauliflower, and kiwi pack a vitamin C punch significantly higher than oranges?

Despite the advantages of these foods over oranges, getting your kid to eat a chili pepper or kale salad may not be realistic.

****

What is the population of Bakersfield, California, and why is it important?

Bakersfield is an oil and carrot town located on the southern edge of the San Joaquin Valley. It has a population of just over 300,000, and a police force that leads the nation in officer involved fatal shootings on a per capita basis.

In 2015, the Bakersfield Police Department shot and killed 13 criminal suspects, while in New York City, a police force 23 times larger than the Bakersfield force, killed 9.

Whether the suspects deserved to die or not is up to the police and courts to figure out, but the numbers are revealing of perhaps a deeper problem.

****

Human beings have five senses: sight, hearing, touch, taste, and smell. Parapsychologists believe we have a sixth sense, called ESP, or *extra sensory perception*. ESP is useful for sensing the presence of spirits, reading other people's minds, foretelling the future, and dealing with the subconscious mind.

ESP is not magic or evil, it is simply a finely tuned awareness of one's environment and a sensitivity to others. In the world of flying fighter jets, pilots think of the sixth sense as *situational awareness*.

****

Beef Wellington is an English meat dish made from a steak fillet wrapped in a pastry and baked. It is most often served with a sauce or gravy poured over thinly sliced portions of the beef with the pastry crust intact around the meat.

The origin of the name Beef Wellington is often attributed to the Duke of Wellington, who played a key role in defeating Napoleon at Waterloo in 1815. However, the concept of wrapping beef in a pastry and then baking the concoction is much older than the Battle at Waterloo, and the actual recipe for Beef Wellington did not appear in print until 1939.

****

The much loved submarine sandwich goes by a lot of different names, especially if you live in the northeastern portion of the United States, where the names of popular food items change by the neighborhood you find yourself walking in.

For example, while visiting Philadelphia, I found bistros, cafes, diners, and taverns selling submarine sandwiches with names like : sub, wedge, hoagie, hero, grinder, and baguette.

It doesn't really matter what you think the right name for a sub sandwich is…as long as you get it right according to the locals.

****

Looking at the possibility of paying child support?

According to family advocate experts, you should expect to pay around 205 of your gross pay for each child not living with you. As a former employer, I made monthly alimony and child support payments presented to me as wage garnishments. The maximum payout allowed by law in my state was 50% of an employee's gross wages.

According to *Forbes* magazine, the legal fees associated with divorce proceedings averages between $15,000 and $30,000. Interestingly, the more times you marry, the higher the rate of divorce.

For first time married couples, the divorce rate hovers around 41%. For second time marriages, the rate increases to 60%, and then spikes to 73% for third times a charm losers.

****

The closest star to Earth is the Sun. Beyond our solar system, you would have to travel for 4.3 light years to visit our nearest neighbor, Alpha Centauri.

A light year is the distance light travels in one year. Since light clips along at 186,000 miles per second, and 6 trillion miles in a year, the distance to Alpha Centauri is over 24 trillion miles. The last time I checked, there are no known rest areas, McDonalds, or factory outlet malls, along the way...so be sure to pack a lunch!

****

Birds have no since of smell...which means they cannot take time to smell the roses. However, from a bird's eye perspective, lacking the sense of smell is convenient when you find a flattened possum carcass on the road, or a fish head floating in the surf.

****

The human tongue can only taste sweet, sour, salty, bitter, and umami.

Umami, as it turns out, is an ill-defined sense of thickness or fullness you get when sipping on a thick creamy soup.

Of all the tastes, umami appears the most important for our early evolution because it told our ancestors whether a particular food was rich in calories, including protein and enzymes essential for growth and good health.

The average human has 10,000 taste buds on his or her tongue. Amazingly, taste buds are fragile, and must be rotated out with new taste buds very two weeks.

Despite the constant rotation of taste buds, our like or dislike for certain foods and taste appear to be imprinted in our memories. If you don't like the taste of something by the time you are three years old, there's a good chance you never will.

However, as we age, the number of taste buds on our tongue tends to decrease, allowing some older people to acquire a taste for strong flavors they may have previously despised. This was especially evident with my father, who ate sauerkraut straight out of the can and preferred a crunchy dill pickle over a candy bar.

If I had known this as a child, I would have asked my mother to hold off on making her favorite dish of cabbage and carrots for those days when most of my taste buds were checking out...but no joy, we ate cabbage and carrots for dinner more often than I care to remember.

****

Have you ever wondered why skydivers and paratroopers shout *Geronimo* when they jump out of their airplanes?

During World War II, paratroopers training at Ft. Benning, Georgia reportedly watched the 1939 film *Geronimo* the night before a group jump.

One of the paratroopers yelled "Geronimo" as he exited the plane in an effort to add levity to the tense training environment. The act became an instant hit with skydivers to this day.

****

What if an airplane flew into a hailstorm?

This is not a good situation, as a pebble or even baseball sized hunk of ice hitting an aircraft at 400 plus miles per hour can be devastating, and may even shatter the cockpit windows as well as deform the leading edge of the wings...leading to the loss of lift (and lives).

Pilots routinely fly around or above thunderstorms, but sometimes the interaction of aircraft with storms is unavoidable.

For example, a microburst, which is a strong downdraft in the swirling winds associated with a thunderstorm, slammed Delta Flight 191 into the ground at Dallas, Texas on August 2, 1985. 136 people lost their lives in this tragedy, causing the aviation industry to install microburst sensors in airports prone to severe storms.

****

The British are fond of the term, *Man Friday*, and use it as a moniker for a personal servant.

The source of the term dates back to the novel *Robinson Crusoe* by Daniel Defoe, published in 1719. When Crusoe befriends a native on the island and promptly cajoles the man into assisting him in surviving on the island, Crusoe gives him the name Friday, because that was the day of the week he found him.

While on the surface it appears Crusoe enslaved Friday, in actuality, Friday owed his life to Crusoe and gladly offered his services to pay his eternal indebtedness.

****

Ever a strong advocate for capital punishment, the United Kingdom permanently banned the death penalty in 1969, following passage of the Murder Act of 1965.

****

Until 2006, it was illegal to have a tattoo in the state of Oklahoma…which is fine, because it is still illegal to read a comic book while operating a motor vehicle.

I've often wondered if this applied to tractors. As a child growing up in Oklahoma I can remember seeing farmers secretly reading detective magazines, featuring tattooed femme fatales, while plowing their fields.

****

Have you ever noticed Americans are in love with suing each other?

A lawsuit is filed about every 30 seconds in America, with half of those being related to cars—as in accidents and sales. Presumably the other half of all lawsuits filed concern dogs and hospital bills.

****

A sign in a community recreation center states: "Drink carefully. Accidents cause people."

But in the world of dumb signs, this one ranks near the top, where it warns motorists of a potential water hazard with a yellow sign claiming, *road wet during rain.*

Another common sign that appears stupid on the surface, is actually sound advice: Bridge Freezes Before Road.

This is true. The air currents that flow under a bridge makes the road surface on a bridge colder than the road surface on solid ground. As a motorist tooling along on a firm road in cold weather, it's good to know the bridge may be covered in a sheet of black ice.

By the way…black ice is not black. It's just a transparent coat of ice that appears black.

****

Henry Ford manufactured 10,666 Model T Fords in 1909. By 1923, that number had peaked at 2,011,125 cars.

In a marketing piece, Ford famously stated, "Any customer can have a car painted any color that he wants so long as it is black."

Ford was also a famous economizer. Parts suppliers were required to ship all parts to the factory in wooden crates of a very specific size. After unpacking the crates, Ford employees disassembled the crates and used the wood for the floorboards on his Model T cars.

Ford stopped making the Model T on May 26, 1927.

****

Soap on a Rope was reportedly invented by the English Leather Company in 1949. During the 1980s it became a popular Father's Day gift, but its initial appeal came as a soap that could be attached to a shower head…in the days prior to the invention of soap holders.

Contrary to popular belief, Soap on a Rope is not a mainstay in prisons, as the rope would be a dangerous item for inmates to possess.

****

What if a champion boxer entered the ring against a mixed martial artist?

Who would win? Well, it depends. In a stand up punch fest, I would put my money on the boxer every time. However, if the boxing match went to the ground in a grappling fest, I would bet on the mixed martial artist who train for the wrestling aspect of fighting—which is exactly why in a street fight I would prefer to have mixed martial art skills over boxing.

According to police and personal defense experts, 90% of every case of street violence goes to the ground in a grappling fest within seconds of the confrontation. Police records also indicate that 23% of the time, injuries sustained in a fight came from a kick, while punching injuries occurred 16% of the time.

The next time you find yourself defending your life on the street, watch out for the kick, and unless you're a good wrestler, be on the lookout for the *takedown*.

Incidentally, outside the ring there is no such thing as a *tap out*. You're in it to win it, or else. And when seconds count, the police are only minutes away.

****

It's been said that in a search and rescue situation, a trained dog is worth 60 human searchers.

In fact, thanks to over 300 million olfactory receptors in a dog's nose versus just 6 million in a human nose, a dog can smell 10,000 to 100,000 times better than a human.

So, the next time you pet your friend's dog, or hold your mom's cat, remember this when you return home…your dog can smell your unfaithfulness before you even open the front door.

****

A clever trick used by editors is to read text backwards to find typos.

This works because the human brain looks for patterns, and will almost always gloss over a misspelled word that looks correct at a glance. Reading the text backwards breaks up this pattern, and forces the brain to piece together the words without relying upon our autocomplete brain skills.

****

It takes approximately 1,600 man hours of labor to build an average size house.

So, what's *average*?

According to the U.S. Census Bureau, the average house size in 2013 was 2,679 square feet. In contrast, the average house size in 1973 was 1,660 square feet.

At the same time, average family sizes have dropped from 3 people per household, to 2.5 people over the same time span.

****

The price of a new home cannot be determined by simply adding the cost of land and materials and labor, but must also include a very subjective measurement of what is known as *added value.*

Nails, boards, and carpet are essentially worthless when looked at individually as items stocked in a warehouse. But when cut and combined according to a plan, the individual components become a home.

Real estate professionals understand this, and encourage home sellers to improve the *curb appeal* of their homes before placing their home on the market. Curb appeal is the overall look and feel of a home that a person gets while driving by your home. Obviously, a clean and well landscaped yard makes a difference, as does the appearance of the front door and trim around the house.

Inside the home, real estate experts advise sellers to bake cookies or place drops of vanilla on a light bulb to enhance the *hominess* of the interior.

In real estate terms, the initial value of your home is typically determined by what the experts call *comps*. A comp is simply a comparison of recent home sale prices in your neighborhood, and is typically based on the sales of three similar homes in your area.

****

If you're looking at improving the value of your home prior to placing it on the market, the most cost effective improvement you can make is to replace the siding or slap a fresh coat of paint on the exteriors of your home, increasing the curb appeal.

Inside the house, your money is best spent on moderate remodels of the kitchen and bathrooms.

However, the worst improvement you can make, in terms of your home's resale value, is in the bathroom. Be careful not to spend a ton of money personalizing the bathroom with your favorite tile, countertops, and clawed foot tubs, as these luxury items are very personal, and will rarely meet the tastes of your potential buyer. A simple remodel to ensure all the fixtures are functional and somewhat up to date is the best use of your money in the bathroom.

You may also want to avoid installing a swimming pool in an attempt to improve the resale value. You are guaranteed to spend more installing the pool than you will see in the increase in your home value.

****

The aircraft used to transport the President of the United States uses the call sign, *Air Force One*. When the president is under the care of the Marines, the call sign becomes *Marine One*.

And just so you'll know, when the Pope flies, his aircraft is called *Shepherd One*.

****

Want to be smarter?

According to scientists, you can increase your intelligence...and it does not involve making a smart choice in your hotel reservation. Instead, try some of these activities: learn a new language, take up a musical instrument, play with puzzles, read books, and get some exercise.

Reportedly, Albert Einstein's IQ was 160. An IQ above 140 is generally considered the genius level, where less than 1 out of every 400 people hang out.

****

Americans own over 96 million cats and 80 million dogs. According to the U.S. Census Bureau, there are 117 million households in America, which means there's a good chance you share the couch and your bed with a furry friend.

As far as dogs go, the Labrador Retriever is the hands down favorite dog pet in America.

****

Professional speakers claim you have to tell your audience something three times for it to sink it. Capitalizing on this, a military curse on public speaking advised speakers to *tell them what you're going to say, tell them, and then tell them what you told them.*

****

Do you love to wear white shoes?

Fashionistas will tell you it is a fashion faux pas to wear white after Labor Day.

****

A typical flour tortilla used to make burritos and soft tacos contains 210 calories, 4 grams of fat, and 37 grams of carbohydrates.

In contrast, a corn tortilla contains 62 calories, 1 gram of fat, and 13 grams of carbohydrates.

****

Never wear red to a funeral in China, as it is symbolic of good fortune and joy…clearly inappropriate! The preferred color of mourning in China is white; whereas in western cultures, black is most often associated with mourning.

****

What if Americans travelled south to visit Canada, rather than north?

Well, if you lived in Detroit, Michigan you would travel south to visit Canada. South of Detroit, just across the Detroit River, is the city of Windsor, Ontario.

Windsor is the only Canadian city south of a major U.S. city in the contiguous United States.

****

What if lawyers were paid by the number of warnings they advised their clients to place on products?

Well, you'd end up with the literal wall papering of products with warning signs. For example, while lifting weights in my local gym, I couldn't help but notice the lat pulldown machine had no less than seven different warning signs, advising me of things like potential muscle pulls, finger pinching, and head impacts.

Considering the risks of weightlifting, I decided to take up rock climbing instead, only to find the park ranger had found it necessary to warn hikers and climbers: climbing on cliffs may result in death or serious injury.

****

Positional asphyxia is a tragic situation where a person suffocates due the position of their body preventing normal respiration. Sadly, death by positional asphyxia is the most common cause of death in chimneys, where people mistakenly believe they can enter a home by way of the fireplace.

Invariably, the culprit becomes jammed in the confined space and suffocates, as in the terrible situation where a female doctor died in 2014 after entering the chimney of her ex-boyfriend's house...presumably to win back his love, or in this case, sympathy.

Useless Dire Warning: Do not attempt to enter a home or building via the chimney. It does not work, and can result in death.

P.S. When you die in a chimney, it usually takes weeks or months for the homeowner to notice the source of the stench.

****

Why are doctors sometimes referred to as *quacks*?

During the plague years in Europe doctors began wearing a duck-billed shaped mask they believed protected them from the disease. It didn't, but the reference to doctors as ducks, or quacks in this case, stuck.

****

A *chimera* is a mythological creature that is a hybrid of multiple animals. The dragon is considered a chimera, and is combination of snakes, raptors, and big cats.

Get used to the word chimera, because it is now being used to refer to sheep and pigs that are being used to grow or produce human organs.

Scientists are using stem cell research and cloning methodologies to implant human cells into the embryos of pigs and sheep. While geneticists claim the resultant adult animals will contain human parts that may be beneficial to human transplant recipients, they also admit the potential for embryonic implants of stem cells can just as easily give the pig or sheep a human brain.

It's all very complicated, and debates about the ethics and practicality of creating chimeras to benefit humans will become a more prevalent part of our day-to-day lives going forward.

By the way, the word chimera is Greek. The *ch* is not pronounced like we would say *church*, but more like the *ky* in the name, *Kyle*. The word is pronounced, *ki-mare-uh*.

****

Speaking of the Greek pronunciation of *chi*, statisticians use a mathematical formula known as a *Chi Square* to measure whether actual, observed events match what the statisticians expected.

A *Chi Square* could then be used to suggest with a probability score that a statistical model or sampling methodology is predictive of real world events.

****

Rats are prolific reproducers.

If a male and female rat were dropped on an island with no rat population, and few predators, within two years the island would be overrun by at least 2 million rats.

No wonder island natives chucked spears at European ships.

Technically, rats typically have litter sizes of 8 pups, and can have 6 litters per year…giving you 48 rats. They are also capable of breeding and reproducing at the tender age of 6 weeks, and have a brief gestation period of only 21 days.

"Holy rat pup, Batman."

****

Speaking of rat pups, did you know the collective noun for a group of crows is a *murder*?

Not to be outdone, we also a *mischief* of mice and a *crossing* of zebras, and if you live in a popular tourist area, you probably already know that tourists come in *flocks*.

****

Domestic turkeys are not nearly as agile or intelligent as their wild turkey cousins. In fact, there have been cases where entire flocks of domestic turkeys have drowned in the rain because they look up in wonderment at the falling water, gawk, and drown.

****

According to the World Health Organization, the leading causes of death around the world include: heart disease, lung cancer and trachea related diseases, stroke, diabetes, AIDS, and road accidents.

In America, heart disease, cancer, and accidents are the leading causes of death.

****

In 2013, 41,149 Americans tragically took their own lives, and despite flu vaccines and advanced medical care, 56,979 people succumbed to the flu and pneumonia.

****

According to the U.S. Census Population clock, the population of America in January 2016 hovered around 322,800,000. Worldwide, the population is currently 7.3 billion.

****

If you're 24 years old, congratulations. In the United States, more people are 24 years old than any other age. The second most common age is 55, which is reflective of the *young* end of the baby boomer generation.

****

California is the most highly populated state in the Union, with 39 million people. As far as density goes, this equates to 251 people per square mile.

Put in terms of people per acre, there are 660 acres in a square mile. So, it looks like Californians get just under 3 acres of land, per person.

****

In 1692, community leaders and zealots hanged 19 suspected witches in Salem, Massachusetts. The original location of the gallows is now a parking lot for a Walgreens drug store.

****

Water boils at 212 degrees Fahrenheit at sea level; but if you plan on making glass from melted sand, you'll have to crank the burner up to 3,200 degrees Fahrenheit.

Translated to Celsius, that's 1,760!

Hot enough to burn the cookies, I can assure you.

****

The Occupational Safety and Health Administration (OSHA) monitors workplaces for hazards to workers' health and safety. While OSHA is often the butt of many jokes (as discussed below in various places), they do manage to make sense every now and then.

For example, according to OSHA, the top 5 work place hazards are: exposure to chemicals, fires, repetitive use injuries (carpal tunnel), electrical hazards, and injury from either falling or having something dropped on you.

****

OSHA claims there are at least 80,000 workplace fires across the country annually. So, the next time your office or workplace conducts a fire drill, pay attention…your job site could be next.

****

The city of Philadelphia requires bloggers to purchase a $300 business license.

****

The largest percentage of people, by age, who visit and gamble in Las Vegas, are over 65 years old. On average, visitors to Las Vegas budget to spend around $600 on gambling, with most of that going into slot machines. Across the country, Americans spend about $40 billion per year on gambling, excluding the lottery.

As for buying lottery tickets, according to CNN, Americans spend over $65 billion annually on lottery tickets. Most states pay a 5% lottery ticket fee to the retailer who sells you a lottery ticket, meaning your local convenience store makes over $3.25 billion per year off ticket commissions.

****

During my first tour of duty in the Middle East, I flashed an *okay* signal to a native by making the o-shape with my thumb and index finger.

I was shocked when the man scowled and stomped away from me. I later learned my *okay* signal was comparable to *flipping him off.*

Cultural mistakes in a foreign land are never good.

****

In Pennsylvania, an old workplace safety rule was adopted by OSHA and enforced as law. Apparently, workers were prohibited from putting ice in their drinks.

The rule was based on common sense, as workers were routinely getting ill from eating ice harvested from contaminated ponds. Pond ice was great for chilling foods before the days of refrigeration, but not for eating or placing in beverages.

****

What's in a name?

Well, according to people who study such things, the most common first names among geniuses are John and Mary.

Sadly, the name *Adicus* did not appear anywhere on this list of genius names. What can I say? It's not my mom's fault she misspelled the popular name, Atticus, from Harper Lee's book, *To Kill a Mockingbird*.

In case you forgot, Atticus Finch played the role of Scout's father in the story. Gregory Peck played a small town lawyer and single parent in the 1962 movie based on the book.

****

In North Africa, the *Eye of the Sahara* is a geological feature of concentric circles measuring 25 miles in diameter. Noticeable only to satellite imagery, the rock formation appears to be manmade.

This amazing rock formation defies explanation, and suggests either alien assistance dating back to an era that may precede the Great Pyramids of Giza, or an incredible geological coincidence.

****

During World War II, nylon used for silk stockings became extremely rare due to the demand for silk used in parachutes.

Ladies desperate to get the *stockings look*, used felt tip markers to draw lines down the back of their calves to simulate the seam in stockings.

****

Why do Brits refer to the toilet as the *loo*?

It's kind of disgusting, but there was a time where people tossed the contents of their chamber pots out the window and onto the street.

A common form of decency was to warn pedestrians below by shouting *garde a l'eau*, which basically means, *look out for the water*.

Translated into English, the Brits abbreviated the warning to simply *loo*, which later became synonymous with toilet.

In another twist of toileting vernacular, the word *John* in reference to the toilet comes from John Harington, a man who improved upon earlier versions of indoor toilets and presented a working toilet to Queen Elizabeth I in the late 16th century.

Three days after delivering the toilet, the world's first case of *plumber's butt* was sighted when a butler was called upon to unclog the toilet.

****

The first official college football game was played on November 6, 1869 against Rutgers and Princeton. The game looked a lot like rugby, with a lot of moving the pigskin on the ground, in a style known as *gridiron* football. About 20 years later a guy named Walter Camp introduced some rules changes that made the game more like the football we know and love today.

As for the forward pass, it was not until 1906 that moving the ball through the air became legal.

Still on the subject of football, the National Football League was created on August 20, 1920. Professional teams represented at the start include: Akron Pros, Canton Bulldogs, Decatur Staleys, Chicago Cardinals, Cleveland Indians, Dayton Triangles, Hammond Pros, Massillon Tigers, Muncie Flyers, Rock Island Independents, and the Rochester Jeffersons.

****

It is estimated that over 60 million civilians died during World War II.

****

The last person to be executed in the Tower of London was a German spy, named Josef Jakobs, on August 15, 1941.

Centuries earlier, Mary Queen of Scotts was beheaded on February 8, 1587 when she posed a threat to Queen Elizabeth I's reign. Sadly, the executioner was a rank amateur and required several swings of his ax to do the job.

Ironically, Mary's son James became king when Queen Elizabeth I died in 1603.

****

In Jared Diamond's fascinating book, Guns, Germs, and Steel, he tells a story of how the South Pacific Islanders responded to the sudden influx of Europeans and Americans on their island.

At first, the islanders asked the invaders, "Why do you white people have so much cargo?" By the end of the war, the islanders had fallen in love with canned corned beef, and even built a stick replica of a cargo airplane, in hopes it would bring the corned beef plane back to their island.

****

Did ever have a fight as kid, and insist your opponent use Marquess of Queensberry Rules?

As a kid we threw that expression around like it was some kind of shield against getting hurt in a fight. In actuality, the Marquess of Queensberry Rules was written in 1867 to establish a code of conduct in the boxing ring.

While the Marquess of Queensberry did not write the rules (that was a man named, John Chambers), the set of rules earned its nickname because of the Marquess' endorsement of the new code of conduct.

Most kids who use the term today think of it as a set of obscure rules of sportsmanship. In my experience, its practical applications meant you could not kick, bite, or use weapons of any sort in a fist fight. Anybody resorting to kicking or using weapons (such as rocks and sticks) was considered a coward.

****

The last president to serve more than two terms was Franklin D. Roosevelt (FDR). He was inaugurated President of the United States four times from 1932 to 1945.

He died in office, on April 12, 1945, just as Hitler's Nazi Germany fell. FDR was replaced by Vice President Harry Truman, who went on authorize the use of the atomic bomb against Japan, effectively ending World War II on September 2, 1945.

Following FDR's death, the 22nd Amendment to the Constitution was ratified, limiting the number of times a person may be elected to President to two terms.

****

The Statue of Liberty cradles what looks like a book in her left arm. In fact, the book is a tablet, shaped like a keystone, and known as the *Tablet of Law*. Inscribed on the tablet in Roman numerals is the date, 4 July 1776.

****

It is yet to be proven, but mathematical modeling and computer simulations suggest a planet 10 times bigger than Earth may be lurking in the outer regions of our Solar System.

Thanks to Pluto's demotion to a non-planet sphere of rock and dirt, the new planet is being called, *Planet Nine*.

****

During World War II a so-called *Dear John* letter was prohibited by law. The military believed a breakup or divorce letter sent to a soldier in the field was detrimental to morale.

If the letter came from a man, informing a female of a breakup or divorce was called a *Dear Jane* letter.

****

In Victorian England, *Resurrection Men* dug up freshly buried bodies to sell to medical schools.

The imagery of digging up bodies and performing experiments on them inspired Mary Shelley to write *Frankenstein*. Mary was also inspired to write the story due to a tragedy. She miscarried and lost a child, and wondered if the growing practice of surgery and blood transfusions may have been helpful.

At the same time, people who feared being misdiagnosed as *dead*, began to be buried with a bell tied to their finger. If they awoke and found themselves in a coffin, the buried alive victim could ring the bell and hopefully draw the attention of a Good Samaritan. Sadly, this practice proved inconvenient when the natural movement of decomposing bodies caused a rash of false alarms.

****

A popular movie starring Leonardo DeCaprio, called *Revenant*, features a mountain man character who survives a perilous encounter with a grizzly, and crawls back to town to confront his friends who left him for dead.

The word revenant means the spirit of a person who returns from death. *Frankenstein* and *Dracula* were both considered revenants.

****

A proposed hyperloop train by inventor and developer, Elon Musk, would send passengers through a vacuum tube at 750 miles per hour from Los Angeles to San Francisco. Your time spent standing in line and clearing security will take longer than the trip itself.

Developers predict the train could be operational by 2018.

****

The Transportation Security Administration (TSA) claims they confiscated 2,700 firearms from carry-on baggage in America's airports during 2015.

No word on what happened to the passengers attempting to carry prohibited items onto airplanes.

Of course, it only takes one case of an illegal firearm finding its way onboard a plane to create a disaster, but to put it into perspective, the Department of Transportation reports over 800 million passengers board planes each year in America…and while most of us experience crowded and over booked flights, in actuality, airline industry watchdogs claim the load factor averages around 82%.

****

What's the difference between a *Tornado Watch* and a *Tornado Warning*? And, what the heck is a *Tornado Emergency*?

A *Tornado Watch* is just a weather advisory alerting residents of a general area that conditions are right for the formation of a tornado. A *Tornado Warning*, on the other hand, is a radar indicated or visible funnel cloud for a specific location. Funnel clouds are unpredictable and may extend damaging tornadic winds to the ground.

The worst situation is a *Tornado Emergency*. In this case, a confirmed tornado is on the ground, and is causing structural damage to homes, buildings, and vehicles.

The tornado that struck Moore, Oklahoma in May 20, 2013, is an example of a tragic Tornado Emergency, resulting in 24 deaths.

****

During the American Civil War, coffee suppliers for the Union Army were so corrupt, they commonly added fillers like saw dust, to their ground coffee mixes. To stop the fraud, President Lincoln required suppliers to ship only whole bean coffee to the troops.

A common sound around camps each morning was a loud tapping, as thousands of soldiers simultaneously crushed their coffee bean rations with the butt stocks of their guns.

****

In the world of gardening, some vegetable crops are known as *companion crops* and get along well with each; while others do not. For example, if you plant peas and onions together, neither one will grow well.

Potatoes are territorial, and rarely do well with any other vegetable crop planted in the same space.

In American gardening three compatible plants, known as the *Three Sisters*, are corn, beans, and squash.

****

The jaguar has the strongest bite of all big cats, and exerts 2,000 pounds per square inch on its prey.

The original name for jaguars, *yaguar*, means, "he who kills with one jump," which is a reference to the cat's ability to kill with a single bite.

In contrast, lions prefer to kill by biting and holding their victims until they suffocate.

****

The average *Facebook* user has 150 friends. Sadly, only 4 of those friends would sympathize with you in a time of need. The rest…well, they just like seeing pictures of what you had for lunch and who you're dating.

****

The famous cowboy actor, John Wayne, was born Marion Mitchell Morrison on May 26, 1907. He died on June 11, 1979.

****

Shield Maidens were female Viking warriors who stood beside the men in battle, apparently performing the same duties as the men.

During the wars in Iraq and Afghanistan it was not uncommon to see female soldiers in gun turrets, as well as other combat related positions. During those wars, 283,000 women served tours of duty in the combat zone, with 800 wounded, and 139 killed.

****

When the crossbow was first introduced into Medieval battlefields, the Pope was so shocked by their lethality, he claimed they were so bad, they must have been created by Lucifer himself.

Although the crossbow was first invented in china around 700 B.C., it was not until the 4th century that the crossbow was employed in Europe.

****

In 845 A.D., 120 Viking ships sailed up the Seine River and captured Paris. They ransomed the city back to the French for over 5,000 pounds of gold and silver.

Apparently, the Viking's primary motive for going into battle was plunder.

****

Finally, an explanation for chronic inertia, also known as laziness…

It turns out some people have a clinical fear of walking, it's called *basophobia*.

****

John Wayne Gacy murdered at least 33 young men and buried their bodies in the crawl space beneath his Chicago home. When not working his contractor business, Gacy could be found entertaining children dressed as a clown…earning him the nickname, *The Killer Clown*.

The state of Illinois executed Gacy in 1994.

****

Bagels are the only bread that is cooked in water. After boiling, the bagels are placed in an oven to brown the crust.

****

If you ever find yourself at the College Inn Pub at the University of Washington in Seattle, look out. The pub is reportedly haunted by a beer guzzling ghost named Howard Bok who was murdered in the hotel above the basement pub.

There are at least 14 pubs with reported resident ghosts in Seattle.

Interestingly, pubs, bars, and night clubs are considered the most popular location for ghost sightings. According to paranormal experts, spirits feed on the energy in clubs, and find inebriated souls easy victims for possession.

If you're looking to find a ghost, don't bother hanging out in cemeteries…go to a bar!

****

The famous operatic singing group known as *The Three Tenors* included, Placido Domingo, Jose Carreras, and Luciano Pavorotti.

Bonus: Top 10 Pub Quiz Questions

If you're looking for an edge in your next pub quiz competition, you would do well to focus your efforts in the following areas that have statistically proven to be popular in pub quizzes around the world. The top ranked categories of questions include: entertainment, history, geography, sports, and politics.

Depending upon where you are at in the world, the most popular pub quiz questions may demand a working knowledge of local celebrities, sports heroes, and politicians…so if you're an American trying to teach a local crowd in London what's what, you better bone up on cricket, soccer (football), and parliament…as well as a national history that goes back a thousand years before Washington threw the proverbial silver dollar across the Delaware.

One of the most common questions asked of pub quizzers goes like this: What manmade object on Earth is visible from the Moon?

The answer is of course: None.

There is a myth going around that you can see the Great Wall of China from the moon, but NASA insists this is not possible without the assistance of binoculars or a telescope.

But for many that may be too easy. In that case, be prepared to answer one of these similar questions…

1. How long, in miles, is The Great Wall of China?
2. What is the only living organism on Earth visible from the Moon?

The answers are 13,170 miles, and the Great Barrier Reef, respectively.

****

A wild man of Russian history named Grigori Rasputin is often referred to as the "Mad Monk" of Russia. Rasputin aligned himself with Tsar Nicholas and his family at a time of great turmoil in Russia, leading up to World War I, the assassination of the royal family, and the Bolshevik Revolution.

It was said Rasputin had the entire royal family under hypnosis, and while this may be far-fetched, he did have amazing physical powers. One of his religious beliefs held that all men's earthly desires should be fulfilled. To that end, Rasputin reportedly organized frequent orgies, and was known for his sexual prowess. Additionally, people of the time believed Rasputin was a faith healer and was able to predict the future.

When his political opponents decided to kill him, Rasputin was fed potassium cyanide, and apparently walked away from a dose of poison considered powerful enough to kill six men. He was then shot in the chest and stabbed…all to no avail. Finally, his assassins chained him and tossed him in the river. When his body was later recovered, the chains had been removed and his lungs were full of water, suggesting he survived the poisoning, the shooting, and the stabbing, eventually succumbing to drowning in a freezing cold Russian river.

While Rasputin reportedly predicted his own death, that was not a big stretch…as it was commonly known, a lot of people wanted to kill him.

That said, expect questions on Rasputin to go like this…

1. Who was the "Mad Monk" of Russia?
2. What year did the Mad Monk of Russia die?

The answers are Rasputin, and 1916, respectively.

****

For some reason questions about Australia are popular in pub quizzes. Leading the charge is the frequent question: What is the capital of Australia?

Most of us unfamiliar with the Land Down Under may jump to the conclusion that Sydney is the obvious seat of government. But we would be wrong. In fact, Canberra is the capital. Beyond this common question you may also expect questions about kangaroos, the Great Barrier Reef, and the meaning of words unique to Australia. Three of the most common questions include:

1. What is the meaning of the word, Australia?
2. Name the Strait that separates Australia from Papua, New Guinea.
3. What was Australia's common name in the 18th century?

The answers are South Land, Torres Strait, and New Holland, respectively.

****

Another popular question in the geography category asks you to identify the source for the name of the Canary Islands.

A good guess may be to adlib about how canaries are plentiful in that part of the world; therefore, canaries must be right. Wrong!

The Canary Islands are actually named after the Latin word for dogs. Ancient Romans travelling to the islands gave them the name Insula Canaria, meaning island of dogs.

On a more somber note, the Canary Islands are also infamous for the location of one of the worst aircraft disasters in the history of commercial aviation.

On March 27, 1977, two 747s collided on the runway at Tenerife North Airport, killing 583 people. Ironically, the KLM and Pan Am planes were not even supposed to be there! They had both been diverted to Tenerife due to a bomb threat at Gran Canaria Airport. Dense fog and a crowded tarmac contributed to a tragic series of events that led to their devastating collision.

Years later, another Pan Am 747 was involved in a bomb related disaster when Pan Am Flight 103 exploded over Lockerbie, Scotland on December 21, 1988, killing 270 innocent passengers, crew, and civilians on the ground.

****

The next question in popularity typically delves into local politics. Here is where you can expect questions about your city council, state and federal government, and current events.

For example, in Britain, a popular question asks you to identify various party leaders, and in the U.S. you may be asked to identify Cabinet members, or Congressional leaders.

****

An old favorite from the entertainment category asked pub quiz competitors to answer the question: Who shot J.R.?

This question was in reference to a popular television show in the 1980s that I never watched, called *Dallas*. I never figured out who shot J.R. because I never watched the show and refused to read the tabloid magazines that featured photos and articles of the Dallas characters every week, for years.

And that's the way it is with entertainment questions. If you asked me about *Star Trek*, I'd be all right. But if you asked me about *Twilight*, I'd lose.

All you can do to prepare for this category is to be aware of what is currently popular. You can't force yourself to watch television shows you hate, or go to movies you hate...all under the pretense of one day being asked a pub quiz question on the stuff.

Instead, just do your own thing, try to keep up with current events, and hope the questions focus on your brand of entertainment.

And by the way...video games offer a new brand of entertainment that many of us older quiz takers know nothing about. So, in your preparations, don't forget to familiarize yourself with popular video game plots and characters.

****

No pub quiz is complete without one, and probably closer to three or four, sports related questions. The key to success in this category is to live and breathe sports. Short of that, you need to at least keep up with team standings and rankings of the top players in whatever sport is currently in season.

A popular question in America asks: Name the one NFL team to go undefeated for an entire season.

The answer is the 1972 Miami Dolphins, who went 17-0.

A bonus question here may ask: Who did the Miami Dolphins beat in the Super Bowl to go 17-0 for the season? The answer: The Washington Redskins.

****

Rounding out this section, here are seven other random questions you may expect in your next pub quiz:

1. Name the world's largest desert.
2. What type of vehicle did Jethro Bodine drive in *The Beverly Hillbillies*?
3. Name the four Beatles.
4. What popular singer joined Mel Gibson in his film, *Mad Max: Beyond the Thunderdome*?
5. How many tentacles does a squid have?
6. Name the three tunnels in the movie *The Great Escape*.
7. Where is Alcatraz Island located?

And the answers…?

1. Antarctica
2. Oldsmobile
3. John Lennon, Paul McCartney, George Harrison and Ringo Starr
4. Tina Turner
5. 10
6. Tom, Dick, and Harry
7. San Francisco Bay

Money Fun Facts

I saved the best for last.

When it comes to facts, and answers to your *What If* questions, your money trumps everything.

Enjoy this collection of random fun facts, and trivia about all things money…

****

When it comes to currency, famed economist and master of money, Milton Friedman, claims, "Only government can take perfectly good paper, cover it with perfectly good ink and make the combination worthless."

****

The DOW Jones Industrial Average (DJIA), is the trademark indicator of the New York Stock Exchange, and is seen as a broad measure of the overall American economy.

The DOW is comprised of 30 stocks: Apple, American Express, Boeing, Caterpillar, Cisco Systems, Chevron, Coca-Cola, DuPont, ExxonMobil, General Electric, Goldman Sachs, Home Depot, IBM, Intel, Johnson & Johnson, JPMorgan Chase, McDonald's, 3M Company, Merck, Microsoft, Nike, Pfizer, Procter & Gamble, The Travelers, UnitedHealth, United Technologies, Visa, Verizon, Wal-Mart, and Walt Disney.

From a statistical and historical perspective, comparing the DJIA to previous years is difficult due to the constant rotation of stocks in and out of the average. The above names were current as of January 4, 2016.

****

The U.S. Census Bureau does a lot more than count heads. It also compiles data on how much money you make, how you spend it, and how you earn it.

One of the top indicators of American wealth is the median household income number. Sadly, this number has been going down in recent years, suggesting the working class people in America are poorer today than they were 10 years ago.

As of January 1, 2016, the median household income in America was $51,939.

By now an alarm bell should be going off in your head, demanding to know more about this thing called *median* income...

****

Statistically, a *median* number is the number where an equal number of the sample population is higher than the median number, and a correspondingly equal number of the sample is lower.

The *mean* is a numerical average of all data points, and a *mode* is a data point that occurs more frequently than any other data point.

Statisticians are famous for manipulating these numbers to present the case they are trying to make. For example, if a survey of 100 people revealed an average income of $52,000, and among those surveyed, 7 people earned over $100,000, a statistician could announce the income mode is $100,000. For people who do not understand the three major measures of central tendency, the mode can present something completely different from reality.

Likewise, if the statistician wanted to present a more negative impression of earnings among those surveyed, he or she could use an average, where a majority of those surveyed earned a very low income. The resultant average, or mean, in this case, would be *skewed* by the prevalence of low income earners.

So, the next time you hear or read a statistic, ask yourself: What are the motives of the organization or government agency presenting this number?

In a personal example, I was once responsible for a military warehouse. During an annual inventory of the equipment in my assigned warehouse, I reported a truthful number reflecting a 99.97% inventory accuracy rate. Behind those numbers, I was missing (later found) a very expensive, controlled item. My commander understood a thing or two about statistics and was not impressed by my extremely high inventory accuracy average, and instead, demanded to see the raw numbers that accounted for the missing .03% of items.

So, when you hear somebody say, "statisticians lie," don't believe it. They're not lying…they're just picking and choosing how to tabulate and present the data to make their case.

This truth is especially relevant when it comes to percentages used in claims of investor returns on investments.

When you see an investment portfolio that claims a 17% ROI, for example, do a little critical thinking. Where and how was the number determined, and better yet, what does a ROI based on past performance have to do with future performance?

You can learn a lot by reading the large print in a contract or prospectus, but your real education is in the fine print…especially when you neglect to read it!

****

For many years Carlos Slim of Mexico has led the Forbes list of wealthiest people in the world. Carlos gained the bulk of his wealth from his control of the Mexican cell phone industry, and is currently valued at $53.5 billion…a mere half a billion ahead of Bill Gates, founder of Microsoft.

So, what does a billion dollars look like?

One billion is equal to 1,000 million, and one million is 1,000 thousands…or about two quadrillion more than my current bank balance.

****

In national terms, the *gross domestic product*, often abbreviated as the GDP and representing the total value of all goods and services produced in a country, of the United States was $16.77 trillion in 2013.

A trillion, by the way, is 1,000 billion.

****

The current debt of the United States is $18.8 trillion, with the number expected to rise to over $21 trillion in the next year, or about $58,000 per citizen.

National debt is often expressed as a percentage of a given nation's gross domestic product. In America, this number is 73%. In Australia and India, the debt to GDP ratio is 52%. The lowest is Saudi Arabia at 12%, and topping the list of debt to GDP ratios is Greece, with a staggering 179% ratio.

****

Medicare/Medicaid takes the single biggest chunk out of the annual U.S. budget, with expenditures just over $1 trillion annually.

****

Americans love to borrow, walking into the carpeted areas of their banks to sign for credit cards, car loans, and home loans to the tune $17.3 trillion. Mortgage debt accounts for nearly $14 trillion of that total, with credit card debt equaling $924 billion, and student loan debt equaling $1.3 trillion.

****

46 million Americans currently live in poverty. According to the U.S. Census Bureau, a family of four earning less than $23,283 is considered poverty stricken.

I wonder how they define people like myself who earn half that and have twice the number of kids.

****

Have you ever dreamed of winning the lottery?

Imagine a world where you had an unlimited spending budget, could buy anything without first checking the price, and could give away a ton of gifts to all your long lost relatives and former classmates. What a world, right?

Maybe not.

For starts, you rarely win the advertised jackpot. First, there's a good chance you will have to share the jackpot with other winners, then there are the taxes, and finally, there's the payout, which may be an annuity over 20 years, or a deeply discounted cash payout.

A friend of mine once won a $3 million dollar lottery jackpot. He took the cash payout of $1.5 million. From that, he paid approximately $800,000 in taxes, leaving him with around $700,000. He used the proceeds to buy a small ranch, a new boat, new truck, and various toys he had long dreamed of owning.

Within 2 years he was forced to sell the ranch because he could not pay the property taxes. To his credit, he knew not to quit his job, and continued to cut hair in a small barbershop.

Incidentally, up until 2016, the largest jackpot ever won was a $656 million Mega Millions jackpot in 2012. In January 2016, a Powerball jackpot reached over $1.6 billion. Three people eventually won the jackpot, netting $198 million each after taxes and taking the cash payout option.

According to the National Endowment of Financial Education, nearly 70% of all lottery winners eventually end up bankrupt.

****

According to Bankrate, 63% of Americans could not pay for a $1,000 medical emergency.

****

Americans give more of their income to charity than any other nation. They give twice as much as Britain and Canada, and 20 times more than Germany. And as far as the American wealthy go, while representing only 1% of the population, over 80% of the money given to charities at death, comes from these people.

****

When looking at potential rental property investments, expect to pay 100 times the monthly rent for comparable homes or apartments in the area.

For example, a home that rents at $1,000 per month would be valued at $100,000. Sadly, vacancies, maintenance, and insurance typically runs at 40% of the gross rents.

****

Stock market investors in America lost $2.3 trillion in stock value during the first two weeks of trading in 2016.

****

Grocery stores don't make as much money as you may think. Sure, their gross receipts may be high, but the average profit margin in the grocery industry hovers between 1-3%. The most highly profitable department within your grocery store is the meat market.

When shopping for your health and your budget, you are best served by focusing on the perimeter aisles, where the produce, meat, and dairy are typically stocked. Prepared and packaged foods, such as cereals, canned soups, and boxed casserole mixes, are typically located in the center aisles.

The best piece of real estate in a grocery store is what grocers call the *endcap*. The endcap is the shelf at the end of each aisle. Grocers often stock sale items and special offers on the endcap to encourage impulse purchases and reduce comparison shopping. Double check the prices for items on an endcap with comparable products on the interior aisles to make sure the advertised deals are true bargains…and not just clever marketing tricks.

****

The Bureau of Labor Statistics (BLS) monitors unemployment in America. As of the beginning of 2016, the unemployment rate is fairly low, at 4.9%.

However, what the BLS does not tell you is how the unemployment rate is calculated. As it turns out, any unemployed worker who exhausts his or her unemployment benefits, or gives up looking for work, is no longer considered unemployed.

These people are tracked in the labor participation rate, which is currently at a dangerously low, 62%.

****

The Villages, Florida residents score the highest average credit rating, at 780 per person. The lowest: Camden, New Jersey, at 566.

Credit scoring is reported using a compiled number credited by the Fair Isaacs Corporation, and known as your FICO score. The number ranges from 250 to 900, with 250 being horrible, and 900 being perfect.

****

For people earning less than $1 million per year, over 50% of them make their money from wages and income. For those earning more than $1 million per year, only 15% claim their income comes from wages and salaries, and cite capital gains from stocks as their primary source of money.

****

To find the estimated market value of any home in America, including your own, visit Zillow.com. Just enter an address to find out where you stand.

****

Here's one of the best money sites on the Internet: **MissingMoney.com**.

Go there and follow the simple search steps to find abandoned bank deposits, unclaimed insurance, etc. There is no fee to use this site…and it works.

Shortly after hearing Oprah talk about this website, my wife entered her name in the search box and discovered an unclaimed life insurance policy left by her father. She was able to recover several thousand dollars from the Missing Money fund (managed by each state), and also alerted several family members that also had unclaimed money on the books.

Check it out, and be sure to search using the various spellings of your name, as well as each state you have lived in. When you're finished, start searching for missing money using your family members' name. They'll love you even more when you tell them where and how they can pick up their unclaimed cash.

56564262R00122

Made in the USA
San Bernardino, CA
12 November 2017